101 Wa

Your Busine~~ ~~~~~~~~~~~~

John Fenton is Britain's best-known sales and sales management trainer. During his year of leadership of the National 'Year of Selling', he was dubbed by the media 'the Billy Graham of Selling'.

But John Fenton is not all showman and business evangelist. He founded the Institute of Sales and Marketing Management (originally the Institution of Sales Engineers) in 1966 and was its Chief Executive until 1984. He is a past President of the Institute of Purchasing Management and was, in the early 1970s, made a Fellow, by invitation, of both the Institute of Marketing and the Institute of Materials Handling.

As a management consultant and non-executive director he spends much of his time in the corporate boardroom, advising on sales and marketing strategy and profit improvement. He is a regular contributor to *Accountancy*, with his own by-line, 'Memo from the Chairman'.

Up until September 1989, John Fenton was Chairman of the Sales Boosters International Group, which included Structured Training, one of the UK's premier sales training organizations, and Sales Control and Record Systems.

In September 1989 he sold his business empire for £10 million and 'retired' at the ripe young age of fifty-one.

Also by John Fenton

The A–Z of Industrial Salesmanship
The A–Z of Sales Management
How to Double Your Profits Within
the Year
How to Sell Against Competition

JOHN FENTON

101 Ways to Boost Your Business Performance

Mandarin

A Mandarin Paperback

101 Ways to Boost your Business Performance

First published 1988
by Heinemann Professional Publishing Ltd
This edition published 1990 by Mandarin Paperbacks
Michelin House, 81 Fulham Road, London SW3 6RB

Mandarin is an imprint of the Octopus Publishing Group

Copyright © John Fenton 1988

A CIP catalogue record for this book
is available from the British Library
ISBN 0 7493 0459 6

Printed in Great Britain
by Cox and Wyman Ltd, Reading, Berks.

Contents

Acknowledgements

Thanks to Andrew Crofts and Joe Windsor
for their input and expertise.

Preface

You are a busy manager – you can't waste time reading long-winded books on the evolution of management, and untested theories of how to improve your performance.

Your life is spent putting out fires, and frantically trying to keep on, near or ahead of your targets – depending on how frightening your boss is.

You're not alone – we're all in the same boat. There's never enough time to think things out and plan really thoroughly, and there never will be.

If I am going to help you be a better manager in this book, I am going to have to work fast in order to hold your attention. There will be no frills, no fancy theories and no waffle. I will be as clear and easy to understand as possible. I will give you blacks and whites, gos and no-gos, rights and wrongs, dos and don'ts, nuts and bolts. I will give you proven ideas that will be easy to put into practice, easy to sell to your boss, to your managerial colleagues and to the troops.

You are almost certainly in a rut, particularly if you have been doing your job for more than five years. If you are the founder of the business the rut is probably so deep you can't see over the sides any more.

You're still not alone. It happens to us all. Ruts start out as fresh new furrows, and it is often hard to tell when you have ploughed too deep until too late.

I held the number one seat in the Sales Boosters International Group since 1966, and I found myself in hundreds of ruts during that time – but I discovered the ways to climb out, and that is what I want to share with you in this book.

If you are now smiling – read on. If your hackles are starting to rise, sell this book to someone else and stay safely in your rut – nobody wins them all.

John Fenton

1

Foundation Stones for Effective Management

In 1984 I wrote a book called *How to Sell Against Competition*. I was honoured to have the foreword written by the Duke of Edinburgh, whose message illustrates precisely where every manager should lay his first foundation stone.

> 'It is a glaring glimpse of the obvious to say that no amount of production is of the slightest value unless the products are sold for cash. Selling is the very crux of any commercial or industrial enterprise.'

So, no matter what kind of business you are managing, one thing is clear:

> **Nothing happens until somebody sells something**

Personally I love signs, and there will be plenty of them throughout this book. Try placing some of them strategically around your place of work – they remind people why they are there. Without reminders they will quickly forget, and allow their personal priorities to take precedence over the priorities of the business.

My favourite sign comes from ex-Avis chief Robert Townsend:

> **Is what I'm doing, or about to do, getting us closer to our objective or making us money?**

He had it next to his telephone, I've also hung it on the back of our executive toilet door.

Each of the foundation stones, which we are listing as we go along, deserves to be inscribed on a sign.

An unbelievable number of companies don't see selling as the be-all-and-end-all of their business. They make things, or set up as experts in providing some kind of service, and then sit back and wait for the customers to come to them – which of course they don't. The result is failure, unless they have enough personal contacts to keep them struggling along as a small company.

If their product is good, professional sales promotion can turn any small struggling company into a large and prosperous one.

Foundation stone number two defines precisely what every business is:

The customers are the business

Without customers you haven't got a business. Any company which doesn't put customers first is doomed to fail. This is so important it warrants another sign. This time, however, the sign is a set of working rules for your business:

A customer

A customer is the most important person in the business – whether he comes in person, writes to us or telephones.

A customer is not dependent upon us . . . we depend upon him for our living.

A customer is not an interruption of our work . . . he is the purpose of it. He is doing us a favour by giving us the opportunity to serve him.

A customer is not someone with whom to argue or match our wits. No one ever won an argument with a customer.

A customer is a person who comes to us because he needs certain goods or services. It is our job to provide them in a way profitable to him and to ourselves.

A customer is not a cold statistic . . . he is a flesh and blood human being, with emotions and prejudices like our own.

A customer is **the most important person** in this business . . . without him there would be no business.

So the customer comes first – not the products or services, or the factory or the corporate image, or the founder or owner of the company. It is the customers which are your business before everything else.

Every activity within your business, therefore, should be measured against how it affects the customers, not how it affects the people working in the company.

Achievement and growth

Every manager should be looking for achievement and growth – which brings us to foundation stone number three.

At its simplest, achievement and growth come as a result of *consistently* giving £1.10 worth of value for every £1 you get from the customers.

To give this kind of value you must manage the business effectively and efficiently. Any sort of inefficiency within the company and you will quickly find that you are giving 90p worth of value for every £1 you get from the customer. If you are in a competitive market – and who isn't – that will mean big trouble.

Marks & Spencer remains the outstanding example of a business that works very hard at giving £1.10 worth of value for every £1 it takes, but there are many small businesses which do the same.

The sign for foundation stone number three, therefore, is:

Always give value

Next we must look at what is sometimes known as corporate style. Good management must always be three dimensional. The three dimensions are economic, entrepreneurial and social.

- **The economic dimension:** This means the professional process of combining commercial, administrative and technical skills and using them to reach profitable objectives.
- **The entrepreneurial dimension:** Originally the word 'entrepreneur' was a French definition for the interface between assets and customers. These days the word means much more than that.

Entrepreneurial management should include unquantifiable ingredients like imagination, energy, risk taking, foresight and the
courage to seize opportunities which other people have missed.
- **The social dimension:** This means balancing the needs of the
  business with the needs of the community – both inside and
  outside the company.

A corporate style should be a mixture of these three dimensions, and
a good manager must quickly identify the proportions of the mixture
in his or her company.

Keep the balance right

Foundation stone number four, therefore, is to try to keep this
mixture right. If it is not correctly balanced you will need to change
your managerial approach until you have restored the equilibrium –
hopefully without treading on anyone's toes in the process.

An accountant, for example, is likely to run a business on the basis
of economic management alone. An entrepreneur might not give
enough thought to the economic and social dimensions, and weak
managers tend to put too much emphasis on the social dimension –
being overanxious not to upset anyone, they will respond to the
pressures of how people feel, without sufficient concern for the aims of
the business.

Once you know what you are looking for, it is very easy to pick each
type out – just try looking around your own management team. You,
however, must strive to be the perfect blend of all three dimensions.

Strategy or tactics

Foundation stone number five is another balancing act. On one end of
the scales is the management of strategy, and on the other the
management of tactics.

Let's define the difference:

- A company's **strategy** is its campaign to achieve long-term aims
  and broad objectives.
- Its **tactics** are the day-to-day nuts and bolts decisions of how to
  reach those long-term strategic goals.

In most companies the directors set the policies and goals – i.e. the strategy – leaving the managers to operate those policies and achieve the goals.

If you are a director, therefore, in a perfect world you should be determining the plan for future growth, and then delegating the actual achievement of the growth to your managers. But how often does that happen?

Any manager who wants to protect his position, needs to master both strategy and tactics.

One problem is that many managers work their way up to their positions through the ranks. They begin by 'doing things', and then start working on tactics when they graduate to supervisory or junior management roles. By the time they reach senior management they are completely accustomed to thinking tactically, having been immersed in the day-to-day problems of the company, and are unable to see the broad, strategic picture.

It is a trap which can be avoided, as long as you are aware of its existence.

A manager, for instance, who is used to operating tactically, might say to his team: 'We need more business, so we'll have to get some more orders.' Everyone then jumps up and down and perhaps some more orders will materialize.

A strategic thinker, faced with the same problem, might say to his managers: 'We need some more business, and to get it we're going to try to take 3 per cent of that market, or we're going to launch into this new market, or we're going to increase our penetration, or we're going to take over this particular competitor.' The increased orders would then follow on from these strategic decisions – provided they were the right decisions, of course.

With strategy you can move your business to a new position in the marketplace:

Know the difference between strategy and tactics

There are two golden rules attached to this foundation stone.

The first golden rule is never to plan any strategy until you have completed a SWOT analysis:

- **Strengths** – (yours and your competitors')
- **Weaknesses** – (yours and your competitors')
- **Opportunities** – (profitability and cash flow)
- **Threats** – (existing and resultant)

You may not be able to see any threats at present, but if you upset the status quo by going for another 10 per cent of a particular market, how are your competitors in that market likely to react?

Strategy is a business chess game, played with real people and real money. You must always think out the consequences of all your moves before you make them.

The second golden rule is never to carve your strategy in stone. If you decide to have a formal 'that's it and that's how it'll stay' plan, it will start to be wrong even while it is being typed up – assuming that it was right in the first place. Every day after that things will happen in your marketplace, both at your competitors and within your own company, which will make your plan even more obsolescent.

Strategic plans should consist of a series of tactics, each of which is flexible and can be changed as circumstances dictate.

The five foundation stones for boosting managerial effectiveness

1   Nothing happens until somebody sells something.

2   The customers come first.

3   Achievement and growth come from giving value.

4   Balance your economic, entrepreneurial and social management mixture.

5   Decide whether you're managing strategy or tactics.

2

Is Marketing Bunk?

Marketing is fashionable, and as soon as anything becomes fashionable all sorts of 'creative' types move in and make ludicrous claims for their own magical powers. There are grains of truth in all their claims, but there is also a lot of flannel as well. So let's define what marketing should be about:

> '**Marketing is the management process responsible for identifying, anticipating and satisfying customer requirements profitably.**'
>
> *UK Committee of Marketing Organisations*

Note those vital words – marketing is a **management process**. It is not a 'phenomenon', or an 'art', or a 'science' – it is a **process**.

Without marketing all you can do is keep on selling the same products and services to the same customers. Inevitably that will lead to you going out of business, because you are standing still while the world outside moves on.

Using the principles of marketing, however, you adjust, amend or change the products or services and the ways in which you sell them, in order to suit the changing needs of your changing customer base. In other words you react positively to the constant evolution of your marketplace.

It is simple to test whether you are marketing, or simply selling. Are you changing anything? Are you seeking new ways to satisfy your customers? If the answer to either of these is 'No', you are not marketing and you will soon be out of business.

Marketing is only bunk when it is applied incompetently. It is also bunk to call your Sales Manager a Marketing Manager, and your Sales Office a Marketing Services Department.

Executives prefer to have marketing titles because they want to be fashionable, but, unless they are orchestrating every facet of your business that affects the customer, they are not marketing.

The Marketing Director is the conductor of the orchestra, the choreographer of the ballet and the arranger of the music.

What business are you in?

Have you ever asked yourself this question? A lot of companies never do. The majority of those that do ask it get the answer wrong, but unless you get it right you can never be really successful.

If you know what business you are in you will be able to see your entire future mapped out before you. You will be able to decide on your direction and development, and you will be able to make sound judgements about your growth potential.

Imagine, for a moment, that you owned a company making horse whips a century ago. If you had been asked what business you were in then, your answer might have been: 'I'm in the horse whip business.' If so, you would today be out of business altogether or catering for a tiny, specialized market. Your products would either have to be incredibly expensive and incredibly high quality to cater for what's left of the landed gentry, or they would have to be cheap and cheerful enough to appeal to riding clubs and school children (and perhaps a few sales managers). Whatever happened you certainly would not have prospered.

Supposing, however, you had answered with: 'I'm in the transport accessories business.' Today you would have a broadly based business selling everything from driving gloves to suitcases, saddlery to bicycle pumps. Throughout the century you would have been diversifying and expanding to satisfy the changing needs of the customers.

Suppose, in today's market, you sell fuel pumps. I ask you what business you are in and you reply: 'Fuel pumps'. That answer may be all right today, while pumps are in demand, but will they be in demand tomorrow? Could advances in technology make your current product range redundant? Might a competitor bring out a radically better fuel pump at half the price?

Had you replied, 'We're in liquid fuel technology – at the moment we sell fuel pumps, but if it concerns liquid fuel then we're interested,' you would not be digging yourself into such a narrow rut, and you would be leaving yourself room to move and adapt to future developments.

Alternatively you could have replied: 'We're in pumps. At the moment it's fuel pumps, but as long as its pumpable it doesn't matter what it is, we'll sell you a pump to pump it.' This is the right answer if you know that your skills lie in the manufacturing of pumps rather than in the technology of liquid fuels. Because you have analysed your strengths you can see more clearly where you can go next.

Another possible answer could be: 'We're in engine accessories. At the moment we only make fuel pumps, but if you can hang it on an engine, it's going to be of interest to us.' Once again you have opened up a range of possibilities for development and growth.

If you can take the broad view of the business you are in, you will be around a lot longer, and you will be a lot bigger and more profitable. You're in energy not liquid fuels, movement not pumps, power instead of engines. These three things – energy, movement and power – are always going to be a viable basis for a business. Who knows how long liquid fuels, pumps and engines will survive before technology replaces them?

The market segment problem

Let's take another example, which will illustrate the problem of market segmentation.

You manufacture fans, and the market is divided into three segments – technical fans, which are complicated and do unusual and clever things; conventional fans, which fill a large proportion of the total market, and cheap and cheerful fans for people who don't care about noise, vibration and product life as long as it sucks fresh air in and blows smells out.

Do the personal interests of your Board of Directors lead you to concentrate on the wrong segment for the good of the company?

Perhaps, for instance, you have a Technical Director who is one of those boffins who yearns for pre-eminence in the field of fans. Despite the fact that you sell your products into the conventional fan segment of the market, he writes the definitive paper for the Institution of Electrical Engineers on an incredible new type of fan which he has invented. He then pushes the company towards projects which are the

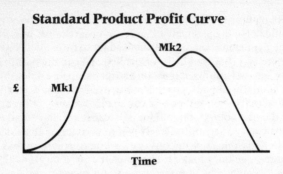

Standard Product Profit Curve

Figure 1

equivalent of Concorde, and commits engineering resources to things that are not part of the company's normal business pattern.

He will beat the rest of you over the head with comments like: 'You known, we really ought to be there. It's good for our reputation,' until eventually you begin to think perhaps he is right and the rest of you are wrong.

If, however, the company isn't tuned up for the high technology end of the market, its people not quite clever or skilled enough, the worst thing that could happen is that you win a contract to supply the Concorde fan. The company could well collapse under the strain of trying to fulfil the contract, simply because of one man's aspirations to make it something which it isn't.

You may also have a Sales Director who is new to the company and believes in 'volume at all costs'. He keeps saying to the salesforce: 'Look, I'm not interested in all these silly little orders that we're getting for twenty-five here and twenty-five there. I know that there's a demand out there for fans by the hundreds of thousands. Go get it!'

Now, however, he has put the company in direct competition with those making cheap and cheerful fans. These people have much lower overheads, and they know how to make things *badly*.

In order to compete you have to have a factory full of people who also know how to make things badly, because at the moment you make them too well for the bulk market.

One of the salesmen comes back with an order for 5000 fans. 'Of course we had to give the customer a discount and he wants a change of spec., and there's a penalty clause . . .' but the Sales Director is thrilled because **'That's volume!'**

The company then ties up its capacity making the 5000 fans, the penalty clause keeps management in a permanent panic, the workforce become fed-up because they're not used to making rubbish, and all your regular customers go elsewhere because they can't get deliveries or service from you like they used to.

Unless your organization is competent and qualified to do it, and you are sure you can make money at it, don't step outside your market segment.

Product life curves

If you are making plans for the future, you must take your product life curves into account. Figure 1 is an illustration of the Standard Product Life Curve.

What normally happens is that the Mk 1 of a product or service is introduced into the market and does reasonably well for a period, then it peaks out and begins to decline.

Shortly after the decline starts, management has a meeting and says: 'We ought to do something about this. What's the cheapest thing we can do?'

The result is a new body, a new shape, a new colour and a new launch for the Mk 2.

'We now have an improved Mk 2,' the salesforce tells the existing customers, and the advertising tells the prospective customers.

So the product life curve is given a boost and they've bought themselves a bit more time. The Mk 3, Mk 4, Mk 5, Mk 6, Mk 7, and Mk 8 all get developed the same way, but it's still the same product and the Mk 1's peak is seldom repeated. Eventually the product hits rock bottom and is removed from the market.

Of course there are many variations to this theme. If we are talking about a good, solid, safe, fundamental industrial product like a valve, the time base for the curve could be fifty years. If we are talking about a motor car, the time base would be more like five years. For electronic products like computers it could be as little as one year, but the principle of the curve remains the same.

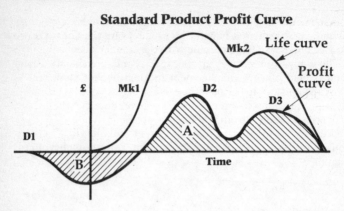

Figure 2

The profit implications

For every product life curve, there is a critical secondary curve, one that the majority of managers never plot. It is the profit curve.

Consider the example we have just drawn up. When the company launches the Mk 1 it is investing money in the product well before the launch date. There are the market research, development, tooling up, advertising and sales promotion costs, all of which are substantial, and many of which will also continue for some time after the launch.

Once the break-even point has been reached through sales, the net profit from the Mk 1 can then be plotted, and the resultant profit curve might look something like Figure 2 when superimposed on the product life curve.

The overall profit achieved by the product during its lifespan can therefore be defined by subtracting shaded area B from shaded area A.

It is easy to see in this example that the product has made little or no profit. The costs of revamping the Mk 1 into the Mk 2 were perhaps too great. Possibly it would have been better to launch a totally new product, while leaving the Mk 1 to decline gracefully – but to still generate *some* profit.

Most businesses have a range of products, and to gain an overview of the whole picture, they need to superimpose all the different product life and profit curves together.

Good managers, therefore, need to keep all the curves moving in the right direction by introducing new products at the right times, so that their future peaks will coincide with the troughs of other products.

The profit budget

A Marketing Director who really wants to earn his corn must be able to blow the whistle on stopping old products and starting new ones at precisely the right times. To identify the right times will require another graph.

Many managers look at profit as 'what's left over at the end of the year'. They either say: 'We had a good year, we've got that much in the bank.' or 'Don't talk about it!'

This approach is fundamentally wrong. In order to manage the affairs of the business efficiently you need to have a **profit budget**. This should be a month-by-month profit target against which you can measure actual performance. Each month you will be able to ask, 'Are we going the way we want to go?' and the answers will be in front of you. It is a profit target instead of a profit statement.

You plot your target profit as a graph, say for each month across three years. Then on the same graph you calculate (and this is the easy bit) the profit you're going to get from the things you are doing **today**.

Profit Gap Analysis

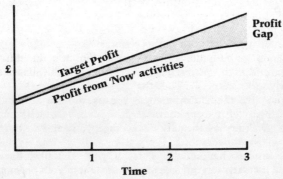

Figure 3

Today's products, today's services and today's markets – and over the three years on the graph you'll invariably get a tail-off.

So now you have a gap between your target profit line and your 'if we stay as we are' line as in Figure 3. If you are watching the extent of the gap it becomes very much easier to determine the points at which you should blow your whistle, and to see at which points you need to make efforts, investments and developments in order to keep to your profit target.

Market development

Whatever your business, I'm willing to bet that there are at least 100 things you can do to develop **new** markets for your existing products.

Good managers read a lot. How much do you read? How extensive is your personal management library? How many newly published books on management, marketing and selling have you acquired in the last year?

If you are going to stay ahead and maximize your effectiveness you need **input**. Articles in journals, books like this one, video and audio tapes, seminars, courses and association meetings all provide stimulation, ideas and information. If you cut off these sources of input your output will soon grind to a halt.

Your USP

This is the most crucial point in this chapter.

USP stands for Unique Selling Proposition. It's the **difference** beween you and all the others. It is the one thing which your salesforce can actually sell.

You must give them a difference, because otherwise they have nothing else to sell except themselves, and if your staff turnover figures are anything like the national average, you will know that you can't rely on that for very long.

Do you know what your USP is? If you do know, have you pin pointed it clearly in your sales literature and in your promotions? Have you trained your salesforce in how to sell your USP?

Once you have identified your USP, you must work out which sectors of the market actually need it. It's no good wandering off into the wide blue yonder stopping everyone you meet and asking: 'Do you want one today?'. If you are looking for growth, extra business and new markets you must work out where they are likely to be, and then present them with the evidence of why they need your USP. That is marketing.

So let's recap, and include three more signs that you can hang around your place of business.

Checklist

1 If you're not changing something, you're not marketing.

> **The only thing in life which is permanent is change**

2 Determine what business you are in, and what segment of the market.

3 Superimpose your product life and profit curves.

4
> **Make your profit *every day***

5 Read at least six new business books a year, and keep the input coming.

6
> **Know and use your USP**

3

The Competitive Picture

Now that you have armed your sales force with your USP, it is time to march out on the offensive. Before you can do that, however, you must develop a clear competitive picture.

When General Montgomery headed the Eighth Army in North Africa during the Second World War, he used a caravan as his desert headquarters. On the wall of the caravan he pinned a picture of his arch enemy General Rommel.

History doesn't relate whether Montgomery threw darts at the picture, or drew moustaches on it, but we do know that he kept that picture there in order to have something upon which to focus his thoughts clearly. He could look at the picture and say things like: 'If I were you, what would I do?' and 'If you discovered I'd done this, what would you do about it?'

Montgomery knew more about Rommel than anyone else, because he had made a very detailed study of his adversary.

You should make an equally deep study of your competition, and it should be a **graphic** study.

If you were to ask most managers: 'What's the competition doing?' you would think you'd asked a rude question. Many of them will get extremely shirty or embarrassed and say: 'Let's not talk about them,' or 'Well, we don't actually have competitors; just a few people who do something similar.'

In business this sort of complacency can be fatal. Maybe managers can take their own people for granted for a time and still survive, but take your competitors for granted and your only chance of survival is that they are **all** worse than you.

Get your picture of Rommel. Get a map of your geographical market, the biggest you can find. Stick it on the wall of your office. Get lots of coloured pins, and stick them into the map. 'Here's our Head Office, our factory, our depots, and our sales people's homes.'

Get some different coloured pins and do the same for each of your competitors. 'That's where their sales offices are, and their factories. Now where do *their* sales people live? Where do they operate from?'

If you develop the big map for each competitor you will see some interesting things. Because you can see the *whole* competitive picture in one go, you may discover that one of your main competitors has ineffective coverage of the South-West. Perhaps they haven't got a depot down there and their nearest sales person works out of Birmingham.

You may never have realized this before. What does it mean? It means that there is a hole in the market in the South-West, an opportunity for you. If you have the capacity for expansion, you can aim ruthlessly at the competition's weak spots, wherever you can find them.

Not only can you plot your competitor's locations and people, you can also plot their promotional campaigns. It can unlock a treasure trove of information. Once you have plotted their advertising and promotional thinking for a year or two you can almost certainly predict what they will do next year, unless they change their whole advertising and marketing team. You will even be able to predict how they will do it.

Piggybacking

A competitor's promotional campaign can actually work **for** you instead of **against** you. If you know it is going to happen, you can ride on the back of it.

Say one of your main competitors launches a major campaign to promote their product or service to chemical engineers. Rather than kicking your desk and shouting: 'Those ••••• have done it to us again!', you increase your **own** activity towards the same target and climb on the bandwagon.

Your salespeople could telephone the same chemical engineers and say; 'There is a great deal of interest currently in the chemical engineering industry about this subject, isn't there?' Having seen the advertising the engineer agrees. 'Yes, I suppose there is'. He doesn't want to be left behind, so your salespeople reap the benefits from your

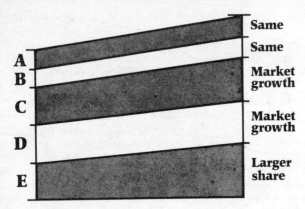

Figure 4

competitor's campaign. It can mean a lot of fun at the competitor's expense – not to mention new business.

All this is possible if you plot their movements, watch it all closely, and work with the information consistently. **That** is how to take your competitors to the cleaners at minimum cost, while having maximum fun.

There are so few managers actually doing all this that I am willing to bet that no one reading this chapter can invite me to his office tomorrow and show me a map with all the details.

The price of penetration

Sometimes the costs of increasing your market share are not worth paying, and you need to weigh up the benefits against the possible losses.

Say, for example, that there are five major competitors sharing a marketplace, A, B, C, D and E. You are E, and you're aiming to increase market penetration during the next year. You want to raise your share of the market at the expense of some, or all, of your competitors.

During the year in question the market itself grows slightly. In graphical form, the situation might look something like Figure 4.

Back at Company E you are aiming to take business away from your competitors as well as getting your normal share of the natural market

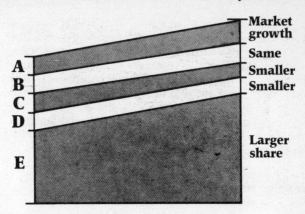

Figure 5

growth. You don't want to win too much at this stage. You don't want to frighten anyone.

At the end of the year the following conversations are taking place in the four other boardrooms. Companies A and B are saying: 'You know, I thought we might have done a bit better this year, but we've managed to hold our own, so I suppose we can't grumble. At least we're no worse off than last year.' Companies C and D are saying: 'Mmm. That's an interesting growth on last year. We must have turned the corner.'

When you have a market share as low as E in our graph, you can go for a modest increase in market penetration, and it's doubtful if any of your competitors will even realize you're winning while they're losing.

But what happens if you already have a more substantial share of the market like Company E in Figure 5?

If you are company E in this situation, and you are aiming to win your natural share of market growth **plus** a larger share at the expense of the competitors, it could be much more expensive.

A, your closest competitor, gets his natural market growth and is happy. B gets the same as last year and comes to the 'could be worse' conclusion. But C and D definitely feel the squeeze, and that means they are going to start paying attention to what's happening.

If C and D start to panic you can imagine one of the likely moves they will make – they may well ruin the price base in the marketplace in their last ditch attempt to stay alive. They will be practically giving the products away, with massive discounts and special offers which none of you can afford to live with.

So be very careful. If you've already got the kind of market share E has on our graph, the effect of going for increased penetration could be to completely wreck the profitability of the market for the next five years.

Maybe it would be less expensive to develop another market where you have a smaller share, but where you can quietly make a lot more money. Or maybe you should acquire C and D.

Your sales strategy

Before you develop your sales strategy, ask yourself one fundamental question. Is your business 'skill-based' or 'asset-based'?

A skill-based company probably has a small core of clever people who design software, create advertising copy or knock down chimney stacks. In that case your sales strategy must be aimed at fully utilizing the skills of these people for the maximum bottom line profit. One of your main preoccupations will be looking for additional market areas where those skills can be employed.

An asset-based business might involve running a hotel, or owning some expensive computer controlled machine tools. So your sales strategy must be aimed at filling your bedrooms and your conference facilities every night of the year, or selling the capacity of your machines so that you can run triple shifts, twenty-four hour days, and six-day weeks.

Both types of business must work towards the same goal – **utilization** – but they will get there in different ways.

Your choice of sales strategy will also depend upon which phase you have reached. Are you, for instance, seeking to establish yourself in the marketplace? Or are you going for additional penetration? Are you trying to reach, say, a 35 per cent market share? Or have you reached that target, and are now thinking about consolidating there and moving on to something else? Are you involved in a change of technology? Do you need a sales strategy that will keep you ahead in a rapidly changing technological, fashion-conscious or similarly vola- tile market?

In the high technology rat race, there are many good reasons why it is more profitable to be the **second** company into a changing marketplace. The market leader will always have the problem of educating the whole marketplace to the existence of the new technology, and of its value compared to what came before. This can be a cripplingly expensive phase.

Once the potential customers have been educated, however, the number two company just comes in and takes its share of the market. It might be a smaller share than number one's but it will be a lot more profitable.

It might be a good time for your company to adopt a sales strategy which simply aims to improve the financial return which you receive from your existing operation. This might require some lateral thinking. Don't take it for granted, for instance, that just because you've always used a particular building, piece of equipment or person for a particular purpose, that you can't use them for something else as well, or instead.

Renovation rates

By renovation rate I don't mean the number of times you redecorate the boardroom, I mean the rate at which a customer buys your product or service.

If you sell toothpaste, the average family might buy your product once a week – that is your renovation rate. If you supply fleet motor cars, the average company trades in its fleet once every two years, so that is your renovation rate.

Every company has one. If you don't know what yours is, you'd better find out – fast. Then use it positively, building it into the sales strategy.

Let's take the motor car as an example. I buy a car about every two years, usually from the same guy. Why? Because he keeps tabs on when I last bought one and he knows my pattern for buying. So two or three months **before** the two years are up he telephones me and says: 'It won't be long now before your car is due to be replaced. I just thought I'd give you a ring because I'd like to bring over the next car which I think you ought to buy, and take you for a spin in it. We'll go and have a beer or whatever.'

He tries to catch me just **before** I start thinking about trading my car in for a new one. As long as he can do that, he's first through the door and in the very best position to win my next order.

With this method you can get the drop on your competitors any time you want to. The strangest part of the whole business is – virtually nobody bothers to do it.

Variety reduction

Are you the kind of business which has a relatively small number of products or services that move very fast, or are you a specialist company which is expected to carry a complex range of alternative solutions to your customers' problems? Perhaps you are a supplier of one unique lump of expensive capital equipment which your customers only buy once every ten years – or perhaps you are somewhere in between these extremes.

The specialist has to carry a wider variety of products than the business working on the 'big store' principle, which would love to be able to offer absolutely no variety at all, just 'as many as you want so long as it is a standard size and standard colour'.

In the real world, maximum effectiveness tends to be a carefully planned compromise somewhere in the middle of all that.

The specialist business has another problem. Its salesforce is probably made up of technical people – engineers for example – and the wonderful thing about engineers is that they will never sell today's products.

They come back to the office after seeing the customers, time and again, saying 'If only it had one bell instead of two, a whistle and three apples, I could sell that to this customer.' So you say: 'All right, all right,' and you take a bell off, add a whistle and three apples and the sales engineer goes back to the customer, comes back again and says: 'He thinks it's fantastic, if only it had wheels.' So you add wheels.

After two years of this your highly efficient specialist business is a disaster area. The costs of your promotional material have gone into orbit, and you are continually having to retrain all your own people. You finish up with a salesforce, an office staff and a production team who don't understand the product range because it's too complicated. So that's the message that comes across to the customers. If you can't train your own people, how on earth can you train the customers?

So don't allow 'specials' unless it is unavoidable and for decent-sized orders – never one-offs.

Always look for variety reductions in your product range wherever possible, and make this a key part of your sales strategy. The results will be cuts in stocks, cuts in training costs and cuts in the costs of promotional material. The range will become easier to sell and you will make far higher profits as a result.

Selling methods

Many businesses allow their selling methods to fall into a rut, and consequently never look at the alternatives – of which there are many.

If you have your own salesforce you could use it to sell direct to **part** of the market. You could then use a contract salesforce to approach a totally separate part of the market. Another part of your product range might be most suited to selling through a distributor, while another might go best through a wholesaler. (The essential difference between a distributor and a wholesaler, for the purposes of Figure 6 below is that a distributor has his own salesforce, whereas a wholesaler just has a warehouse.)

You might also like to consider franchising, and overseas sales through licensing agreements rather than agents.

Figure 6 illustrates the main options.

Should you change the status quo?

Once upon a time there was a very well-known, well-established British firm called the Dictaphone Company. Like many other companies in their field, their salesforce always sold their dictating and intercom equipment direct to the end users.

Gradually the costs of selling rose, and Dictaphone found that it couldn't sell any more to the first-stage user – that is the customer who only wanted one dictating machine and one transcription unit – because the value of the order wasn't high enough to cover the cost of the salesperson's calls. So the sales force stopped selling to first-stage users and concentrated on the users who might buy large numbers of units, such as major companies and local councils.

SELLING METHODS

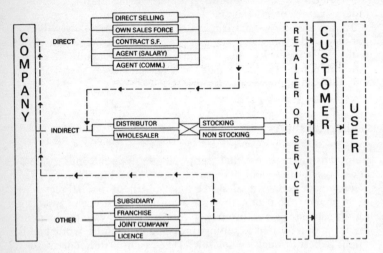

Figure 6

None of this happened overnight, but Dictaphone slowly found that as the costs rose, it was cutting itself off from the starter end of the market, so that when its past customers came back two years after the initial purchase, asking for a Mk 2, or a repeat order, they couldn't handle the business.

They had to change their tactics fast, setting up a network of distributors to handle the bottom end of the market before they were forced out of it altogether. They were virtually the last company to recognize the need to do this. So when they finally got around to setting up distributors they found that all the best ones were signed up by the competition.

They only just sorted it out in time, and have since done a good job of rebuilding their former position in the marketplace. I bet that is one mistake they will never make again.

Let this be a warning to you. Think about tomorrow. If you haven't changed the way you sell in the past five years, even in some minor way, you may well be missing a slice of the market altogether, or paying far too much for the way you are currently reaching your market.

Checklist

1   Instigate a graphic study of your competition.
2   Try some piggybacking instead of always striving to be first.
3   Establish the price of increased market penetration.
4   Develop your sales strategy:
   - Skill-based or asset-based.
   - Use your renovation rates.
   - Examine and update your selling methods.

4

Improving Performance

Have you got a giant club, with nails sticking out of it? It is, after all, the traditional management tool for improving the performance of people at the 'sharp end' – i.e. the salesforce – metaphorically speaking, of course.

Big stick managers like to threaten people – usually with the sack – if their performance doesn't improve fast. But by 'performance' they nearly always mean 'results', so they haven't even got that much right. In fact they've got it all wrong.

Performance has to be measured within a clearly defined time span. Results, which generally means the number of orders won, do not often coincide with the period in which the performance actually improved.

There is always a delay between an initial enquiry and the confirmation of an order. It could be days, it could be months.

This time gap, during which results catch up with performance improvement by passing through the natural business cycle, can give impatient sales managers nasty heart conditions. If they are bad managers this is when they reach for the big sticks, and people get fired.

At the other end of the bad management spectrum, we have the 'Daffodil Man'. He is usually an introverted but good and sincere salesman, who has been promoted to the sales manager's seat because the previous incumbent got an offer he couldn't refuse, and it was the line of least resistance – and the cheapest way of plugging the hole.

Daffodil Man wouldn't dream of wielding a big stick. He still sees himself as 'one of the boys', and is keen to stay mates with the people he now has to manage. It's doubtful if he will ever receive any management training, even if his ego would allow him to admit he needed some.

His style is 'buy them all daffodils and hope they'll work better'. Nobody gets fired. Nobody gets counselled. Nobody risks offending anybody, or rocking the boat. The business may go bust, but nobody's going to get sacked until the receiver takes over and pushes the button.

Something new

So how about breaking the mould and trying a new way of improving performance? Here are a few resolutions you could make to become a more effective manager.

Take a look at your sales graph for the past year. The trend was probably upwards, and hopefully there weren't any price increases to fudge the figures. The budgeted sales graph was pretty steady, as usual, and continued upwards just sharply enough to keep the top brass happy, but not enough to give you future problems having set yourself a difficult precedent to follow. The actual sales graph, of course, zig-zagged all over the place as usual like Figure 7. Wouldn't it be wonderful to be able to smooth those zig-zags out?

Have you ever investigated deeply why those movements above and below the budget graph keep happening? Some of them might be the results of seasonal demand, or perhaps an expected big order was delayed. There are many superficial factors which can contribute to

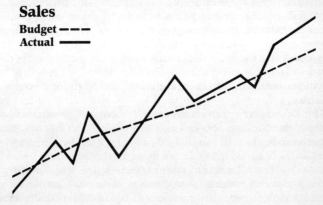

Sales
Budget − − −
Actual ───

Figure 7

the fluctuations, but there is one universal cause which underlies them all, and which many managers choose to overlook.

The fact is that none of us can sustain personal pressure for more than a few weeks before having to pull back for a little R & R (rest and recuperation). After a couple of weeks' break we are then ready for another bout of pressure.

During each period of recuperation, of course, there will be a downturn in business done, and then there will be two or three weeks' delay before the results will come through on the graph.

The pattern of the zig-zags is very repetitive. That is because people's memories are very short indeed. Not only are they unable to work under pressure for any length of time, they also forget what happened only a couple of months before.

Smoothing out the bumps

A good manager has to find a way of sustaining the performance of his team so that it follows the steady line of the budget graph. He also has to boost their performance to keep the line straight and high.

Let's look at half a dozen ways in which you can achieve this.

First take the word 'Ask'. That's three letters, 'A', 'S' and 'K'. Multiply them together and you have Activity × Skills × Knowledge. These are the three key areas of any salesperson's job.

The **activity** is the number of calls he makes, the times at which he gets up in the morning and goes to bed at night. It is the number of hours each day he spends in a layby eating sandwiches and doing his reports.

His **skills** are the hours of persuasion which he puts in, sitting across the desk from customers and potential customers, his ability to ask questions, obtain information, close a sale and all the other techniques of selling.

The **knowledge** means knowing all about the product, its applications, the back-up services and everything else that you need to know in order to talk intelligently to people in the business world. This is where a good manager can make all the difference.

To be successful a salesperson needs to know what the customer needs and wants, which means understanding his business and his markets. He also needs financial knowledge in order to understand the small print of hire purchase and leasing agreements, and the way in which the customer's finances are likely to work. Finally he needs to be knowledgeable about the competition.

If a manager lets anyone loose on his most valuable asset – his customers – without an adequate amount of knowledge in all these areas he deserves to go out of business – which is what will happen very fast indeed. An ignorant salesperson will be able to kill customers so fast you won't even realize it is happening, until too late.

The onus is on managers to ensure that their people receive all the necessary knowledge, and that they continue to receive new information which they can test and experiment with. They may only use 20 per cent of what you give them, but you must continue to supply 100 per cent.

A solid base of knowledge will give them something to fall back on, to sustain them through the pressure periods, and keep them effective even when they are not firing on all four cylinders.

Getting the money right

How do you pay your salesforce? If you pay them commission only it is probably time you changed the system. The ideal, in my experience, is a salary-plus-commission system.

The salary must cover the basic costs of living plus about 10 per cent more. Commission should be payable not on all sales, but from about 80 per cent of the target upwards. Once they reach 100 per cent the commission rate should increase, perhaps it should even double. At 110 per cent you could probably afford to double it again, since you are almost into pure profit by this time.

Always set honourable targets if you want them to work. You must have the commitment of the people who are going to do the work for you, and you won't get that if you set unreasonable targets which they have no hope of reaching.

If you get all these ingredients working together you will have a much steadier sales graph, I guarantee it.

It is important not to keep moving the goal posts for your people by increasing the targets simply because business is getting better. That has the effect of making your top performers start at square one again each year. If a salesperson is helping you to build your business, you must reward him fairly, or you will lose him. The only reason to change the targets from which commission is paid is because of price increases.

If you have a commission-only salesforce, the *ASK* formula might be the best one for you. If, for instance, you grade your people's performance on a scale of 0 to 3, new recruits will start at 0 in the activity, skills and knowledge areas. By the end of three months you might expect them to graduate to level 1, and the formula will then come into operation to tell them how much they are going to earn at the end of the year, presuming their performance stays at that level. It will be $A1 \times S1 \times K1$, which equals 1 if you multiply it out.

Let's take a real-life example of a salesforce in which $1 = £4,000$ a year. That doesn't sound like enough to live on, of course, but the company in question expects that after six months, and the appropriate amount of training, the recruits will be up to level 2. So that makes their earning capacity $A2 \times S2 \times K2 = 8$, and $8 \times £4,000 = £32,000$, which is more than fair pay for most people.

In this particular salesforce there are also some very high fliers, who have reached level 3. If you multiply $3 \times 3 \times 3$ on the ASK formula you get 27, and $27 \times £4,000$ is £108,000 a year.

In reality what happens is that when the salesforce reach points of high pressure, just before they go into the R & R mode, they slacken off on the A section of the equation. So someone who is normally at the 2 level, finds himself on $A1 \times S2 \times K2$. So instead of a formula of 8, he has a formula of 4. If his R & R period lasts a few months that might reduce his earnings from £32,000 to £16,000 a year.

On the same criteria, if the high fliers have a few idle months, bringing their equation down to $A1 \times S3 \times K3$, they will end up with £36,000 a year rather than £108,000.

Hopefully, once they have got used to the top figure, they will not feel inclined to let it slide for very long.

Once the sales force realizes how simple it is to work to the formula, they will all be able to see which direction they've got to travel in, and they will inspire themselves with the necessary self-motivation.

Making them make commitments

Another way of sustaining performance, and consequently improving it, is to redesign your customer records so that the salesforce work to what is called the 'objective and date of the next call'.

What happens is that at the end of every customer call, your salespeople agree an objective and a date for the next call, hopefully while still face to face with the customer.

They enter the information into the record in front of the customer, reinforcing the impression of professionalism, and once back in the car they refile the customer record according to the date of the agreed next call.

Once your salespeople have made that commitment they will have to honour it, and can't 'put off' the repeat call simply because they don't feel like doing it that month. Again you have helped to smooth out some of the troughs in your sales graph.

The next suggestion is so important that it deserves a sign.

Numbers not words

All you can do with words is read them, take the appropriate action and then file them. At the end of each week that is all that can happen to written reports from the 'sharp end' of the operation.

If you are hoping to build a picture of any kind of trend, or a projection into the future, you've got to dig out all the other reports from past weeks and lay them end to end, reading them all again to see if you can spot anything. That is making life very hard for yourself indeed.

Numbers are so much easier. You can do anything you like with them, including sticking them into the computer, and that is the first rule – don't rely on your memory, because no one has a memory which is that good.

Multi-facet monitoring

The graphs and charts in Figure 8 (on page 32) make up an action plan using numbers to improve and sustain performance.

If you look carefully at some of these numbers you will see that they illustrate another important rule when it comes to managing salespeople, and that is 'never set big targets'.

Unless the circumstances are extraordinary, never say, 'Come on fellows, we're looking for a 50 per cent increase in sales next year. You

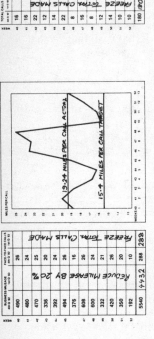

Figure 8

This example is reproduced by kind permission of Sales Control & Record Systems plc, Royal Leamington Spa, Warwickshire CV32 5JH

can do it.' Because they will walk away muttering: 'Daft idiot' and give up before they have started simply because it looks impossible.

Always break your main targets down into a number of smaller ones, each of which will seem like a piece of cake to the sales force, something easy for them to get their teeth into.

If you look at the second and third columns of the repeat business chart you will see the fourteen abortive, useless and no-interview calls which this particular salesperson suffered in the three-month period.

So, one of the twenty or so little targets which you set could be to see a reduction in the number of abortive calls for the next three months, from fourteen to ten.

A reduction of four, after all, doesn't sound too difficult. But supposing you had said: 'We want you to reduce your abortive call ratio by 30 per cent – that doesn't sound quite so easy does it?

Numbers can simplify everything, and that is what multi-facet monitoring is all about. It can, however, be as sophisticated as you need it.

You can monitor the performance of individuals simply by comparing their personal figures, ratios, and the norms of the company. You can measure by exception, saving yourself an enormous amount of time. Anything that is going wrong will show up in the figures.

You won't have time to measure everything, so you look for variances, which will show up clearly, allowing you to take fast action to avoid the downturns on the graph.

With a system like this it is easy to set small, attainable, quarterly targets, either for each individual or for the whole team. Once you have set the ball rolling you can sit back and watch things automatically moving in the right direction. The team will be able to see for themselves how well or badly they are doing. They will soon see when they are not coming up to scratch in certain areas, and will usually work to put things right themselves before you have to say anything.

On-the-job training

Many managers find on-the-job training a continual source of embarrassment. Ideally they should spend at least one day a month out in the field with each of their salespeople, assessing, appraising, encouraging, motivating and improving each individual's performance.

They are not there to prove that they are better at selling than the person they are managing, and may even have to sit quietly and watch while orders are being lost before their very eyes. (Not many managers can live through this. A prior agreement system of signals is better – salesperson rubbing left ear with right elbow means 'Help me out, I'm struggling' etc.)

The embarrassment often comes between the manager and the managed because nobody has bothered to spell out the detailed objectives of the day. If both of them are clear about what is expected of them, it all starts to happen.

We have developed a system for field appraisals which monitors a salesperson's personal selling standards and performance record. The whole system is illustrated in Figure 9.

The manager has a marking sheet, providing the basis for assessment. It carries separate columns for 'Above Standard Performance' (A) 'Standard Performance' (B) and 'Performance Needs Improvement' (C). In each column are statements relating to twenty-four different aspects of the salesperson's job.

The manager has one of these for each of his salespeople, and they each have copies, so that they can see how they are being judged. Every time they both go into the field together, the manager awards marks of either A, B or C, with the agreement of the person being assessed.

It may not be possible to mark all twenty-four aspects in one day, so you must agree together which ones are appropriate. You can then say: 'Right, you've got seven Cs, so our top priority for next month is to improve in those seven areas before we meet again.' That will lead to a month-by-month improvement, and within six or twelve months both you and the people themselves will be able to see some major differences.

It's always very easy to claim that you are too busy to undertake exercises like this. That is just an excuse. If there is a way of improving performance and you shirk it, you are failing as a manager. Your best people will soon sense that you are not on top of the job, and they will start to leave.

There is an old quotation which sums up an important message with regard to performance.

> **We judge ourselves by what we feel capable of doing, while others judge us by what we have already done**

FIELD ASSESSMENT FORM

PERSONAL SELLING STANDARDS AND PERFORMANCE RECORD

Salesperson

CONFIDENTIAL

Structured Training plc

Concorde House, 24 Warwick New Road, Royal Leamington Spa, Warwickshire CV32 5JH
Telephone: 0926 37621-6 Telex: 317488 Fax: 0926 311316

Figure 9

SELLING SKILLS

		ABOVE STANDARD	STANDARD	NEEDS IMPROVEMENT
1	**PLANNING PREPARATION** a) Information	Has all the relevant information for every call	Has most of the relevant information for every call	Has some relevant information for most calls
	b) Sales tools	Always carries all relevant equipment, stationery etc.	Invariably carries some relevant equipment, stationery etc.	Often carries some relevant equipment, stationery etc.
	c) Action plan	Always prepares detailed action plan	Invariably prepares action plan	Often prepares an action plan
2	**APPROACH** a) Opening remarks	Always gains attention by using skilful opening phrases and "carrots"	Occasionally fails to gain attention because of failure to use "carrots"	Seldom uses "carrots" or skilful opening phrases
	b) Sales aids	Always uses a sales aid where appropriate	Often uses a sales aid in approach	Seldom uses a sales aid in approach
3	**PRESENTATION** a) Product knowledge	Fully conversant with all products and applications	Well informed about all products and applications	Has some knowledge of most products and applications
	b) Selling points	Knows and uses all selling points for all products	Knows most selling points for all products	Knows some selling points for most products
	c) Buyer benefits	Always translates selling points into benefits	Occasionally fails to translate selling points into benefits	Sometimes translates selling points into benefits
	d) Buying motives	Always makes presentation appeal to buyers motives	Occasionally fails to make presentation appeal to buyers motives	Often fails to make presentation appeal to buyers motives
	e) Sales aids	Always uses them to maximum advantage	Always uses them, often to maximum advantage	Sometimes uses sales aids, to advantage
	f) Handling objections	Always handles objections successfully, leaving the buyer satisfied	Handles most objections successfully leaving the buyer satisfied	Handles some objections successfully, does not always leave the buyer satisfied
	g) Selling sequence	Always uses correct sequence	Often uses correct sequence	Seldom uses correct sequence
	h) Rental	Always endeavours to sell Rental	Often endeavours to sell Rental	Seldom endeavours to sell Rental
4	**CLOSING THE SALE** a) Buying signals	Always recognises and acts upon buying signals	Occasionally fails to recognise and act upon buying signals	Often fails to recognise and act upon buying signals
	b) Method of Close	Always uses the most appropriate style of close	Occasionally fails to use the appropriate style of close	Often fails to use the appropriate style of close
	c) Departure drill	Always thanks, reassures or questions buyer as appropriate	Occasionally fails to thank, reassure or question the buyer as appropriate	Often fails to thank, reassure or question the buyer as appropriate

ADMINISTRATION SKILLS

	ABOVE STANDARD	STANDARD	NEEDS IMPROVEMENT
5 CALL ANALYSIS a) Records/reports and Correspondence	Always completed accurately, promptly and up to date	Occasionally fails to complete accurately, promptly and up to date	Always completed but not always accurate, prompt and up to date
b) Information	Always records information for future use	Occasionally fails to record information for future use	Sometimes records information for future use
c) Self analysis	Invariably analyses personal performance	Often analyses personal performance	Seldom analyses personal performance
6 TERRITORY MANAGEMENT a) Use of selling time	Plans very carefully and wastes no time	Plans carefully, and wastes little time	Does not plan, and wastes time on unnecessary journeys
b) Competitors Activities	Actively seeks relevant information and keeps everybody informed	Generally good at reporting information	seldom reports competitor activity
c) Territory Development	Constantly active and opening new a/cs in addition to developing existing a/cs	Developing existing a/cs and occasionally opening new a/cs	Inclined to concentrate on existing business seldom trying to gain new customers
7 PERSONAL a) Appearance	Always exceptionally well turned out, and a credit to the company	Always well turned out and a credit to the company	Not always well turned out and a credit to the company
b) Attitude	Always expresses a positive attitude towards the company its products, policies, and its customers	Occasionally fails to express a positive attitude towards the company its products, policies, and its customers	Often expresses a negative attitude towards the company its products, policies and its customers
8 OTHER RELEVANT POINTS			

ON-GOING PERSONAL SKILLS RECORD

By using the Performance Standards as a guide, rate performance under the following headings:
A = Above Standard   B = Standard   C = Needs Improvement

1 PLANNING PREPARATION														
a) Information														
b) Sales tools														
c) Action plan														
2 APPROACH														
a) Opening remarks														
b) Sales aids														
3 PRESENTATION														
a) Product Knowledge														
b) Selling points														
c) Buyer benefits														
d) Buying motives														
e) Sales aids														
f) Handling objections														
g) Selling sequence														
h) Rental														
4 CLOSING THE SALE														
a) Buying signals														
b) Method of Close														
c) Departure drill														
5 CALL ANALYSIS														
a) Records/reports/correspondence														
b) Information														
c) Self analysis														
6 TERRITORY MANAGEMENT														
a) Use of Selling time														
b) Competitors' activities														
c) Territory Development														
7 PERSONAL														
a) Appearance														
b) Attitude														
Appraisor's Signature														

At the end of each appraisal day, the Field Sales Manager should complete this form, with the salesperson discussing the various areas where improvement is necessary in relation to the day's work. The Field Sales Manager should give recommendations and guidance on how the agreed weaknesses should be improved.

For the manager and the managed to understand what the other one is thinking, and to decide what you should think about them, you need a high degree of empathy.

Checklist

1 Are you a big stick manager, a daffodil man, or an **effective** manager?
2 Improve total performance, not just results.
3 Smooth out the zig-zagging sales graph.
4 Work out the $A \times S \times K$ equation.
5 Get the financial rewards right.
6 Get the sales force to make future commitments, chasing **business**, not just customers.
7 Use numbers not words.
8 Set small targets.

5

Watching the Bottom Line

Why are so many managers bad at thinking and talking about profits? Without them we can't fund growth, development or replacement. Most sales managers, for instance, have sales reported to them by the unit, or by the sales value, but rarely in terms of profitability.

Let's take the question of volume first. There are three key areas here which have to be controlled:

- Total
- Rate
- Mix

Imagine that your target for this year is a quarter of a million pounds. That is your **total**. It is vital that you reach the target because any shortfall will result in a disproportionate drop in profits since you can't cut down on your costs. It doesn't cost marginally less in office rents or salaries just because you have failed to reach your targets by 10 per cent. Most of that 10 per cent will hit the bottom line.

To cloud the picture you then have to consider cashflow. This is your **rate**. It may not be good enough to make a sale worth £250,000 if the whole amount is paid in one lump sum a month after the end of the quarter – your creditors may have put you out of business by then. Salaries have to be paid along the way, materials have to be bought, investments made in equipment. So you need to bring business in at a steady rate, not in jerks and starts – and that includes August and December, when people are supposedly on holiday or sleeping off the effects of overeating, because you still have to meet the monthly bills.

Finally you have the **mix**. Profit margins are never the same on any two products or in any two markets. You could have your sales force running around at full speed, bringing in mountains of new business, all of which produces very low profit margins. You may get the total right as a result, you may even get the rate right, but because the mix is wrong there is nothing left for the bottom line.

Managers, therefore, must know exactly what the profitability is on everything that goes out from the company. The more profitable elements of the mix might be the hardest to sell, but they have to be planned for.

Make your profit every day

This merits a large sign. It must be a cardinal rule for every business, and there are many large companies whose accounts departments actually calculate their profits on a daily basis. They find it concentrates the mind wonderfully.

If you are working by the year or the month, and a few days get lost because of a conference, or a clearing out of the filing cabinets, it doesn't seem too important in the overall scheme of things. If, however, you are aiming to make a profit each day you will pay very close attention to the ways that everyone is spending their time – including you. In other words, never let a day go by!

Putting things right

So what happens if things are not going right on the bottom line? What can you actually do about it?

The first thing most of us turn to is cost reductions. It is always a boring subject and nobody likes tackling it, but there are always reductions which can be made if you look hard enough.

Next you look for ways to increase sales. Even in the worst of times there is business out there to be won, it is just a question of working out how to do it.

It may also be possible to increase the profit margin on certain sales. In some cases it is simply a matter of putting up the price or examining your discounting systems. We will cover both these areas in more detail later.

Use your assets

Another area worth studying is 'asset utilization'. It sounds like the sort of thing accountants drone on about at great length, but it should actually be a vital part of every manager's brief.

The obvious assets are the ones which appear on the balance sheet like stock, equipment and machinery. People are also assets, but they are not always taken into account when a company is being valued. Do you, for instance, have someone buried in the filing department who could make a brilliant telesales person? Make sure you are using all your people as effectively as possible.

Your customer list is also an asset. If you are only using it for mailings once or twice a year, invitations to exhibitions, statements and possibly Christmas cards, you are not utilizing it to its full potential. Put some thought into other imaginative ways in which it could be working for you.

Cash management

The way you handle the daily flow of the cash, both inwards and outwards, can make the difference between staying in business and not. The money passes through many different sets of hands and departments in most companies. Is there, for instance, a way of speeding up the flow of money? Could you get cheques paid into the bank a day or two earlier? Could you persuade customers to pay up more promptly? Could you persuade suppliers to wait longer for their money, or to agree discounts for fast payment? Always be sure that you have explored every possibility.

If you concentrate generally on cutting costs or raising sales you are giving yourself a major task. If you tackle one specific thing in each of these problem areas each month, you will find that there is a steady and noticeable improvement in the overall performance of the company.

Financial control

The longer you leave it, the harder it is to keep control of any situation. If a small damp patch appears on the wall of your house and you deal

Moving annual total

The MAT is simply the sum of sales for the past twelve months. Thus, the MAT at the end of March is the sum total from 1 April last year to 31 March this year.

When April figures become known, they are added on, and those for April last year are subtracted from the total.

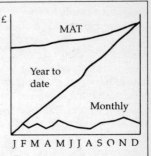

Project the trend

For a first estimate of area sales for next year, project the MAT line.

This assumes that all factors affecting sales trend remain unchanged:

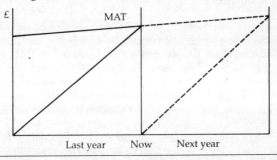

Figure 10

with it immediately, the costs are negligible. If you leave it for a year, you may need a whole new wall, or the house might even fall down.

Likewise, if you only look at the accounts once a year, you may find that the only thing they tell you is that you went bust eight months before, and that the figures have only just come through.

Information is the most valuable asset you can have in any situation. Simply having it, however, is not enough. You must **use** it. If you have figures, for instance, then turn them into graphs. Give some shape to those endless columns of numbers, and keep your eye on the moving annual total (MAT) (see Figure 10).

Each month take your sales figures and add them on to the figures for the previous eleven months, so that you always know accurately what your current annual sales figures are. That is your MAT, and that way you won't be able to coast along on last year's wonderful figures. You are looking for a constantly and steadily ascending line and you will be alerted as soon as a downturn starts to show itself.

Knowing the MAT will also help to iron out the extremes, both upward and downward. These figures are the most sensitive possible indicator of the true state of affairs.

It is also vital to be able to have figures to hand whenever you need them. If you have to make an important decision today, you don't want to have to wait until the end of the month, when you get to see the regular figures, before you can make a decision. The MAT total will tell you exactly what you can and can't afford to do.

What is a budget for?

Most managers hate budgets, when in fact they should regard them as allies. Budgets are simply yardsticks by which you can measure the performance of your people and your business. You need to have budgets for income, for expenditure, and for everything which contributes to the bottom line. So always make sure that you have your own yardstick which accurately reflects your situation.

Sometimes it helps to view your situation from a different perspective. Instead of thinking of everything in terms of money, for instance, try seeing it all as percentages. Instead of viewing salaries as so many thousands of pounds per month going out, look at them as a percentage (say 10 per cent) of sales. It will help you to see if you are in the right ball park, and will be a less emotive way of viewing certain sensitive areas. If you can see that the percentages are drifting up, you immediately know that you are doing something wrong and that your bottom line is being affected.. It means that you can begin pressing alarm buttons much sooner than would otherwise happen.

While you're looking at the figures, it's worth seeing if you can spot any deviations – say any changes of 5 per cent or more.

If you are working from annual results you won't see anything until too late. You could work from receipts for the money actually paid into the company, which will mean you are working slightly further ahead since there is probably at least a two month lead time between the sale being made and the money being paid. Or you can measure from the time of billing, but that is as far ahead as most accountants will let you look. For them nothing counts as real money until it is invoiced.

For the alert manager, however, there are many earlier indications of the way things are going. You might receive despatches a week before the invoices go out, for instance. You could start measuring performances on orders received. Some of them may get cancelled, of course, but in general the figures will tell you whether things are getting better or worse.

To move even further forward, you could measure the numbers of quotations or proposals issued. Of course not all of them will turn into real business, but from experience you will have a rough idea what the percentage rate of conversions is.

If, for instance, you know that one in four proposals converts to business, you know that you will need £400,000-worth of proposals if you are to expect £100,000-worth of business. Because it takes two months to turn a proposal into an order, you have another two months in which to take avoiding action if something is starting to go wrong.

To take it one stage further, you may even be able to measure prospecting, provided you have an idea of the conversion rates involved. If you know that you need to see ten people to win two pieces of new business, and you need two pieces of new business a week to meet your targets, you had better ensure that you see at least ten qualified prospects each week.

To revert to the metaphor of the damp patch on the wall – if you regularly check the guttering for blockages, you may not need to spend any money on repairs, and you will avoid the damp altogether. By keeping a tight control on all the possible indicators of trouble, you can see it coming soon enough to get out of the way.

Delegate to the end of the line

It is often possible to delegate budgets a long way down the line, although there is a widely held misconception that only senior managers can handle them.

In one company which I know about, they put this to the ultimate test. Everyone in the company complained about the standard of the tea served up on the tea trolley towards the end of the week. On Thursdays it was only just drinkable, and on Fridays it was unbearable. For the first three days of the week everything was fine.

So they called in the tea lady and asked her what she thought. 'Simple,' she said, 'there isn't enough tea. I've been telling management that for weeks. I've asked and I've asked, but no-one will give me any more tea. By the end of the week we are running out, so I have to do the best I can.'

They could have said: 'Find a better way to make the tea or you're fired,' but they decided instead to put her in charge of the budget. They gave her all the money which the company and staff contributed to the service, and told her to run it the best way she could. There was no reason why she shouldn't be able to handle a budget. She was, after all, a wife and a mother, and she ran her family very well on a budget, so why should she not be able to run a tea trolley? She certainly knew a lot more about the subject than anyone in management. From then on the complaints stopped dead. At Christmas she had the trolley decorated like Regent's Street. 'Where did all the decorations come from?' the managers asked. 'From the money I saved from the budget' she replied.

So the moral of this story is, push budgeting as far down the line as you can. If, for instance you have a clerk whose job it is to place orders for stock, he will probably do the work in dollops. It is a boring job, so he will push through it all at once and then go back to staring out of the window. The result is an ordering pattern which goes in fits and starts, and a cashflow pattern which follows it.

It is up to management to explain to that clerk about the need to incur expenditure on an even basis, forcing him to rethink the way he does his job. All you have to do is give him a reason to change his ways.

Never waste your time looking at unmarked figures. At some time we have all been presented with those great lengths of computer print-out, bursting with figures. If someone thinks it is worth giving you the stuff, ask them to underline or ring the bits which they think are interestingly high, low or whatever. There is no reason why you should be put to the test of trying to spot the interesting points. By making this a golden rule you will save yourself a great deal of wasted time.

Profit improvement programmes

How can a sales operation develop a profit improvement programme? (Apart from reading my earlier book *How to Double Your Profits Within the Year*.)

You could begin with some small price increases. Will the world really stop buying your product or service if you put the prices up 1 per cent. If you do that you have sent that 1 per cent directly through to the bottom line. If your profit margin is 10 per cent of sales you have increased your bottom line by 10 per cent in one move.

Is there room in your range for some new products which can command premium prices? It might be a new up-market product, or it might be a regrouping of existing products in an up-market package which you can reprice at a higher level.

Are there any add-ons or accessories to your standard range which you could start selling? In some cases the accessories can earn more than the original product. If you are selling someone a shirt, isn't it worth trying to sell them a tie to go with it?

There may be a way of improving the packaging to cut costs and raise sales. Is it possible to package several products together instead of selling them singly, for instance?

There are certain best-selling products which will sell almost anywhere. Ladies tights manufacturers, for instance, seem to cater for a seemingly limitless market. So whatever you are selling to ladies, why not offer to sell them a pair of tights while they are there, and if they are going to buy one pair, why not suggest they save time and buy two? Because they know that they will always end up needing them, women will often take advantage of an offer like that. That is only one, simplified example, but the principle can be extended to cover many product lines and sales situations.

The next target is discounts. Whatever your policy is on discounts, rethink it. Unless there are valid savings to you, it might not be worth giving the discount. If there are valid savings, then it isn't strictly speaking a discount any more. If, for instance, you can save £85 by delivering a whole vanload of product to one drop, and it takes 100 products to fill a van, then there is no reason why you shouldn't offer the customer £85 if he orders 100 instead of the eighteen he originally intended buying. That way you are not offering a percentage discount. You are merely passing on a saving.

Many big companies seem to automatically expect that they will get a discount simply because of their size. If they are going to place huge orders then that's fine, but often they are merely using their size as a bargaining ploy and have no real intention of ordering large quantities. The way round that is to agree to retrospective discounting. If, at the end of the year, they have bought a certain amount of product, then they can have their discount.

Let's look at an example of discounting at work. Supposedly your sales are worth £100,000, and you make a 10 per cent profit of £15,000. Someone then suggests that you should give everyone a 5 per cent discount in order to boost sales. So that brings your original profit down to £10,000, and you have to do £150,000-worth of business to get back to where you started. Do you, in all honesty, think that a 5 per cent discount is going to lead to a 50 per cent increase in business? Even if it does you will have increased your paperwork as well as the amounts of product which need to be shifted around from A to B. Always be very wary of offering discounts.

When did you last look over all those little extra charges that you make: minimum order charges, delivery charges, packing charges, installation charges, commissioning charges. It may be that many of them are now far too low. Perhaps you could increase your minimum order charge by £5 without anybody even noticing.

Going back to the total, rate and mix topic. Have you thought recently about changing your product mix?

We have talked about the differing profit levels on different product lines, so how about changing the mix of products while you are at it? To start with, if you are carrying some loss leaders in the range, think about scrapping them. Some companies are selling products which they don't even realize are loss leaders – which is even worse than doing it deliberately. Are you sure that they are bringing in enough business to make them worth continuing?

The volume trap

Whatever happens you must never fall into the volume trap. More sales volume is not necessarily an improvement. The costs in the form of the price cuts needed to win the business may not be practical to start with. You may even need to put up costs in order to meet the increased overheads of a larger production run.

By changing to volume sales you may increase market resistance, and you will certainly increase competitive resistance.

Instead of going for volume increase which may destroy your bottom line, why not think in terms of an increased range of products or services. Try to broaden your customer base, rather than concentrate the buying power into the hands of a few of your existing customers. Always look for increased profits before increased volumes.

Three break-even charts illustrate the point (Figure 11). The more you sell the further your sales graph rises. The costs are divided into two categories – fixed costs (buildings, investments in equipment, staff salaries and so on), and variable costs like raw materials. The more product you make the more variable costs you incur.

If you add the two cost lines together you can see how much volume you have to produce in order to break even.

If you then increase sales volume you might have to hire another salesperson or another clerk, or buy another machine or delivery van. So even your fixed costs have had to rise to support the increased production. You then get nasty kinks in your graph lines.

All this means that you end up having to push the sales up even higher in order to do more than break even. You must ask yourself if (a) it is worth doing and (b) if the company is capable of making the necessary leaps forward. If the answer is no to either question you could end up making less profit than if you had never won the orders in the first place.

You may, of course, be able to lower your variable costs by buying raw materials in greater quantities, in which case increased volume may be a path to increased profits.

Which of the three types of break-even chart in Figure 11 most closely fits **your** business?

Growth on a zero budget

This may sound like a contradiction in terms, but when it works it is wonderful. It really just means being more successful at improving performance ratios without increasing cost budgets.

Let's look at the way you do things now. You have forty reasonable prospective customers, and you know that your conversion rate is

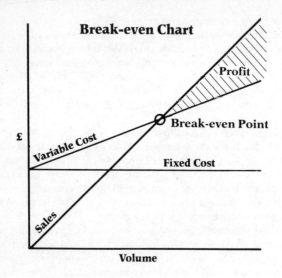

Break-even Chart

Variable Cost

£

Fixed Cost

Sales

Break-even Point

Profit

Volume

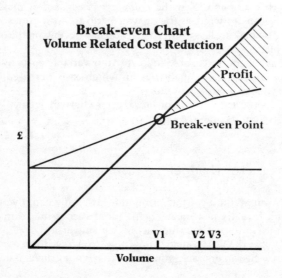

Break-even Chart
Volume Related Cost Reduction

£

Profit

Break-even Point

V1   V2 V3

Volume

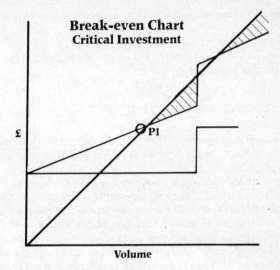

Break-even Chart
Critical Investment

£   P1

Volume

Figure 11

usually four to one. So you should end up sending out ten proposals, quotes or estimates.

You also know that you generally close one in five pieces of quoted business. That means that out of ten proposals you will end up with two orders.

In order to improve your hit rate you must either choose your prospects more accurately, so that they are more likely to convert and you will waste less time on people who won't be interested, or you must do a better job of selling to them. If possible you should do both.

If should not be unreasonable to be able to improve the quality of the prospects so that the ratio changes from four to one to two to one. If you can achieve that, the original forty prospects will give you twenty proposals and four orders.

You then move on to the second step, which is to improve the five to one ratio of proposals converted to orders. If you manage to improve the techniques for preparing the proposals and closing the sales you might change that ratio to three to one. So you would then be able to turn the twenty proposals into seven pieces of business –

which is nearly four times the amount of business you were achieving originally.

All this is possible, of course, only if you have analysed your ratios in the first place. Only by knowing what your shortcomings are, can you hope to improve your performance.

Cutting costs and trimming fat

Most managers are terrible at this. It is, after all, an unpleasant thing to have to do. It has to be done, so what are some of the less painful ways of going about it?

When somebody leaves, for whatever reason, find out if they really need to be replaced. Take the opportunity to look at the whole structure. It's like one of those puzzles where you move all the little squares around, because you have one blank square in the middle. Without the blank square everyone is stuck in their positions; once the hole has appeared, however, you can move anyone anywhere. See who can be moved around to create an organizational advantage out of a loss.

Try reviewing all your sales methods, to see if you are going about things in the least expensive way possible. Should you, perhaps, give some of the product range to a distributor and only keep some of it yourselves?

Analyse how much it is costing to get all the work done within the company. Do you know how much it costs you to produce an invoice, or to formulate a proposal and put it in the post? What to you looks like a few sheets of paper may have cost anything up to £50 once you have worked out the time you took drafting it, reworking it, typing it, binding it and posting it. If you know this, and are happy about the cost, that's fine. If you haven't worked it out before, you may be in for a shock. It may even be that the £50 proposal was for a piece of business which would only have made you £30-worth of profit.

You can then look into the alternatives, which generally means mechanizing or simplifying certain features of the system.

Many companies, for instance, keep a spare driver on the pay roll. Because you have the driver you have to give him a van, and because you've got the driver and the van sitting there you find things for him to do, like running up to the bank, making small deliveries or going out for people's sandwiches. Supposing you were to find something more useful for the man to do, sold his van and used a firm of couriers to do the running about when necessary?

There will be a number of advantages. To start with people will think twice before paying out for a courier, where they wouldn't hesitate to ask the spare driver to do them a favour. You will also be able to keep a tighter control on the way things are done, seeing exactly who is spending what on which services.

Increase the ratio of salespeople

Are you certain that you have the ratio of salespeople to non-salespeople right? It is all too easy to allow the numbers of administrative staff to rise and rise in relation to the numbers actually out in the field doing the bit that *really* matters.

It might also be worth looking at ways of cutting down people's expenditure. Rather than taking somebody's bill and saying: 'There's a bill for £9.32, I'll give you the money,' why not try giving everyone standard allowances for things? Lunch, for instance, when someone is away on business is always £X, and they can work out for themselves if they want to spend any more. If they want to spend less and keep the money for themselves – so what? – it's still cheaper for you than having to pay up more than the standard amount, not to mention all the management time wasted on working out people's expense sheets – £9.32 here and £3.59 there. Just tell them that you don't care where they spend it, that's what they are getting.

Hotels are a major source of expense for any company which keeps a number of employees on the road. The standards of service, however, especially among some of the smaller, privately-owned establishments, have been improving enormously in recent years. In many cases they are good marketeers and will be happy to arrange special deals for anyone who promises them regular repeat business. So ensure that you are getting all the deals you can and are spending your money as constructively as possible.

Business entertainment is the easiest thing to cut right out of the budget. In my experience it seldom achieves anything – except hangovers for all concerned.

Although the telephone is a great time-saver in many ways, it can also be a great time-waster if used badly, and an enormous waste of money. Try attaching a call-logging system onto your exchange which will give you a computer print-out of all the numbers which have been called, the extension they were called from and the cost of the call. Make sure everyone knows you are doing it, and, believe me, you will see your phone bill cut by half overnight. Even if people aren't actively abusing the system by calling spouses, lovers and dentists all day long, they just aren't conscious of how much unnecessary phoning they are doing. Make them think about it.

Are you under-utilizing your women

Most women in business are grossly under-utilized, being left in the corner to do the boring, repetitive jobs that the men can't be bothered with. They often have an intellectual capacity far above the tasks which they are asked to perform. In many cases they are far better than their bosses at performing their jobs. Some men of course can't face the threat of giving women more responsibilities, but it is their companies which suffer as a result.

Recycling your assets

Where are your assets? Are they locked up in empty warehousing space, office space, stock, promotional material, machinery, information or people? It is probably a combination of most of these things. Is there any way you could be using them more effectively?

For instance, try calculating the profit you make per square metre of office space. Then, whenever someone comes to you with a bright idea for moving to bigger offices, or building a nice shiny new block, you can do a quick sum on the back of an envelope to find out if it would increase the profit per square metre. If the answer is 'Yes' then go for it, if 'No', then don't let them talk you into it.

If you can increase your stock turn-round you are improving your use of capital. Just increasing the rate isn't the only thing you can do, however. Analyse very carefully which stock is moving and which isn't. There is often a lump sitting in the middle of the warehouse which never gets any smaller, while all around it things are moving in and out quite nicely. If you can identify where this immoveable lump is, you can get rid of it and use the money more constructively.

Promotional material is another area of enormous potential waste.

Colman's Mustard used to claim that they made their profit not from mustard which you eat, but from the mustard you leave on the side of your plate. I believe that printers make their money not from the material which you distribute, but from all the boxes of leaflets, price lists and other bumf that are collecting dust in the corner of everyone's store cupboards. Every company I know has boxes full of last year's price lists and leaflets for products which they no longer make. If it's too late to do anything with it, throw it out, but it would be better to use it up before it goes out of date. It's an asset, so turn it round.

Checklist

1 Get the **total** – **rate** – **mix** right.

2 Make a profit every day.

3 Improve the bottom line with cost reductions, increased sales and increased profit margins.

4 Use your assets to the maximum.

5 Speed up your cashflow.

6 Predict as far ahead as possible.

7 Use your budgets constructively.

8 Delegate budgeting as far down as possible.

9 Never waste time looking at unmarked figures.

10 Improve profits with price increases, new products, improved packaging and by cutting discounts.

11 Avoid the volume trap.

12 Turn more prospects into sales.

13 Cut costs by painlessly cutting staffing levels, and changing sales methods.

14 Standardize and rationalize expenses.

6

Cutting Down the Admin.

All administration is an overhead, it is up to you to keep it as low as possible. Start with a completely blank piece of paper and say to yourself: 'If I was starting from scratch, how would I do it?' Then write down what you are trying to do, who you are selling to, and the ideal way in which you would start again, knowing what you know now. The chances are that the answers you come up with will be very different from the way in which you are currently doing things. That gives you a good starting point.

Next, look at the document flow within the business. That will tell you how efficient your administration is. Don't produce a fancy diagram, full of little boxes and arrows. Just get the actual document and pin it on the wall with all its copies. Then look at it, and consider where all the copies have to go and why. It may be glaringly obvious that some people who receive copies don't need them.

When TV-AM first came on the air, they had to fill in twelve separate forms about each guest who came on, covering every imaginable thing about them. The whole operation could have been done on one document. The company was very soon in trouble, and has since streamlined itself and prospered. It is all too easy for an administration system to grow like Topsy. Always ask yourself: 'Why do we do that?' If the answer is 'Well, we always have,' you know you have found something which you can improve.

Upgrade your equipment

How many outdated pieces of equipment are you hanging onto, simply because they still work? No doubt that old typewriter is perfectly good, but have you thought about all the other things you might be able to do with a more modern one, or with a wordprocessor? Have you worked out the time which all your staff might save if they had better tools to work with?

A lack of investment in new equipment has often been cited as a major cause for Britain falling behind the rest of the world in the 1960s and 1970s and a contributor to the long recession which we went through in the early 1980s.

That is now largely a historical problem, thankfully, and British industry is, on the whole, aware of the need to invest for the future in order to keep ahead of the competition. Anyone who doesn't learn from the past, however, is making a big mistake. Never under-invest in equipment.

Waste data

Take stock of the data which you have within the business. We have already discussed the under-use of customer lists, but what else have you got moulding away in your files, which should be out in the sun, working for you? Your company records must be full of the names and addresses of people who did business with you in the past, plus innumerable other details about their businesses. This is all valuable sales data – don't waste it!

Time management

Time management is another fashionable management topic at the moment, but the majority of people in business still don't practise it wisely. Most of us do some tasks simply because we always have. So analyse what everyone does, how long it takes them to do it, and whether there are any better ways of going about things.

At each stage of the day, ask yourself: 'Is this the most profitable thing I could be doing with my time at the moment?' If it isn't, then change it.

Go in for a little 'value engineering' or 'value analysis'. Whatever the job, whether it is making a product or managing a factory, you could always do it better. It means looking at each function and asking: 'What is this department, or this product part doing, that could be done in a different way? Can we achieve the same results less expensively?'

Determine what the function is first. Then work out how much it costs. See if you can eliminate the whole thing, or redistribute it. List the alternatives open to you, and consider ways in which you can improve the quality of the process and the results. You might find, for instance, that by improving the quality of the materials or equipment or staff used, you can reduce the effective costs of doing the job.

Differentiate between staff and line management

Staff people and line people are totally different, with totally different characteristics. A good manager must know which of his staff are effective as line managers and which of them are effective in staff functions.

Line managers are very good at people management, and at managing tactics, whereas staff people are much better at strategy and project planning and execution.

Every company needs one person to look after staff. One is nearly always enough, and if you don't watch them carefully they multiply.

You should also analyse your own span of management. How many people do you have reporting to you as a manager? There is a limit to how many you can deal with effectively, so ensure that you are not overstretching yourself.

The way to avoid this it to delegate some of the supervisory and managerial responsibilities within your chain of command. If, for instance, you find you have fourteen people reporting to you, and you think five would be a more realistic figure, then rearrange things by promoting some of your people to take responsibility along the way. By delegating certain jobs clearly, you also cut down the amount of confusion and potential conflict over duties. Don't widen your span of control beyond your capabilities.

Future staffing structures

It's a good idea to keep in your bottom right-hand drawer an outline of a possible future staffing structure over the next one to five years.

Although things change rapidly, you need to have an idea in your mind about who will be at the top of the business in a few years' time. If you know that, you can ensure that the right people get the right training for the future, both on and off the job. That means the external courses on which you send them, and the projects on which you ask them to work within the company. If you know who you need most for the future, you can take extra precautions against them becoming dissatisfied and leaving you. You will also be able to see where the likely future gaps will be, and can consequently recruit in plenty of time. It always takes time for people to find their feet in a new company, and to become effective in their jobs, so you need to have advance warning.

Recruitment is a dangerous game, with about a fifty-fifty success rate. If you have given yourself some time you can afford to make a few mistakes. If you wait until the last moment you might not be able to afford such a luxury.

It is always better to be able to groom the top people up from inside the company, giving them plenty of time and space to make the mistakes necessary to gain experience. Good judgement is frequently the result of experience. Let them make their mistakes in a safe environment, under your control.

It might be worth looking into different ways of using your people. Have you, for instance, thought of setting up special task forces and teams to handle particular jobs? You pull together a team of people from different areas and say: 'Look, here's the problem, our delivery is appalling. We get a lot of complaints about it. What's the matter with it? Where does it go wrong?' Or, 'We have a problem with this particular product or that particular market. You are a team, I want you to work on the problem and see what you come up with.'

By doing this you give people the chance to try different types of work, and it gives you a lot of feedback about the potential for leadership of all sorts of people who haven't usually got leadership or management responsibilities. It also gives them a break from their normal jobs and they can return to the routine later, greatly refreshed.

You will be surprised at the variety of ideas which a project like this can throw up. You might not like them all, but that's not the point. The point is that you are generating some original thinking. The team will be a tool for getting the job done, and also a way to train people for broader management roles. This is so important, it deserves another sign:

Everyone works for the business

In other words, they don't just work for their department, and they don't just process paper, they are part of the whole business.

While we are on the subject of teamwork – what about your right-hand person? In most cases this means a lady, whose job description is typist, secretary or PA. How do you relate to her?

The first rule is never to cut corners when hiring this person. The better they are at their jobs, the more freedom you will have to do yours. Once you have hired them, use them as widely as possible. They are not just typists or filing clerks, they are there to help you to be a more effective manager. 'PA' is therefore a better job description of the sort of person you should be looking for.

So if you haven't already done so, train your right-hand person to make some of your decisions for you. Make sure she is able to write letters herself, so that you don't have to dictate every word to her, and don't have to sign everything that goes out of the office. If you have to prepare a lot of reports in your job – and what manager doesn't – why not let her collect all the information for you?

Once she has been writing letters and gathering information for you for a while, is there any reason why she shouldn't actually write the reports herself? Even if you produce the final thing – that is after all your job – she can do 99 per cent of the work for you. Whereas the monthly report was a constant nightmare to you, it now appears on your desk on a Monday morning for you to make a few corrections before the final copy is printed up.

If you are unsure how to approach this problem, just try asking her tomorrow morning what she would like to be doing, and what she feels she would be capable of. The chances are she will talk for an hour.

Drowning in paper – how not to

Most of us have trouble controlling the flow of paper around the office. There are some ground rules for keeping control of the situation. Start by making appointments with your paperwork just as you make appointments with customers or anyone else.

Then ask your PA to sort through it before you get to it, throwing out the absolute rubbish and grading the rest according to whether it is 'trivia', 'serious' or 'urgent'. Then deal with it group by group. Take the urgent stuff first and deal with the trivia at the end.

Above all, encourage the kind of communication within your company which requires fast, simple answers.

Try using 'ping-pong' memos, for instance. You hand-write a note to a colleague, keeping a copy in your file. He then hand-writes his reply on the back of the same memo, keeping a copy in his files. It saves time and money. Some things of course are not so simple.

Always take action

Watch yourself next time you are sorting out your post. There are always those difficult items which you try to hide in the middle of the pile somewhere, telling yourself that you will come back to that later. Always take immediate action, whether it means making a phone call, or pulling out a file. If you don't you will waste time worrying about what to do, when in fact it could be cleared off the desk in a minute.

The quickest way to drown in paper is to have your own pet subjects – 'I like to deal with that myself' – rather than dealing with things strictly in order of priority. If your PA understands what those priorities are, then she will be able to present you with the work in a logical sequence.

Office status symbols

There is a world of difference between pretension and significance when it comes to status symbols. Pretension is bad, but the respect accorded to a leader, manager or supervisor reflects on the members of his team. People who work for managers can be very sensitive about the respect which is shown to that man by others. It is something which affects the whole group.

As far as office design and allocation of pot plants goes, every company has to decide what is appropriate to their situation. When it comes to things like loos or canteens, however, if one is significantly better than another, you need to improve the bad one rather than relegate it to being a negative status symbol.

Remember that managers aren't the only ones with names. We all like to hear our names and see them written up. Yet many companies which have managers' names and titles emblazoned on their doors, allow the rest of the staff to wallow in anonymity. To make a status symbol out of something like a name plate or decent lavatory is counterproductive.

It is also a mistake to allocate office equipment solely on the basis of seniority. Just beeause someone is very junior, or very new to the company, it doesn't mean that he can manage on a minute desk with jammed drawers and a leg hanging off. That man may have to handle large spreadsheets or diagrams, or may have to talk to clients at his desk. He needs equipment which is suitable to the task, not just to his lowly status.

The same applies to cars. Just because one salesman covers less distance than another, due to the geography of his area, is there any reason to give him a 1.3 litre thing that virtually grinds to a halt on steep hills, while his colleague has something with 4.5 litres which never gets out of third gear?

The advantages and disadvantages of open-plan offices have been discussed in depth for over twenty years now. There are always occasions when people need to be able to talk in private, but the British habit of walling managers in is not a good idea. Managers need to know what is going on, and to be part of it all. They shouldn't be separated off from the place where the work is actually being done. A compromise can sometimes be effectively achieved by simply knocking a few windows in the office wall.

Computers

There is no longer any choice in this matter, all managers have to have a computer of some sort. There is simply too much data around these days for it to be handled any other way. You can't hold it all in your head, and you certainly can't contain it all on paper.

Many companies have mainframe computers which can't be used for specialized purposes due to lack of processing time or lack of software. It would be cheaper to go out and buy your own machine than to hire another clerk or typist to handle the extra data just for you, whether it is producing proposals, next month's visit lists, MAT graphs or your costs as percentages.

You can even ask the computer to do your dirty work for you. How about some computer-generated debtor notices like:

Dear Customer

I am the Universal Widget Corp's computer. May I draw your attention to the overdue balance on the attached statement. So far only you and I know about this, but in 7 days time I am programmed to tell the credit controller – why should we involve him?

Checklist

1 Always have the best equipment available.
2 Improve your time management.
3 Differentiate between line and staff people.
4 Plan future staffing structures.
5 Set up special task forces.
6 Make more use of the women in your company.
7 Get the right right-hand person.
8 Cut down on the paperwork.
9 Make status symbols practical.
10 Get yourself a computer.

7

Finding and Keeping the Best People

If you could invent a business which didn't need people, you would have eradicated most of the problems which beset most of the managers most of the time.

The snag is, of course, that without people you have no business. So the first thing you have to do is ensure that you get the best people possible on your team. The right people will be the ones who work for the furtherance of the business before their own self-interests.

When you go out into the recruitment market looking for people, remember that you are *selling*, not buying. It's easy to get that wrong. To illustrate the point, let's look at two different recruitment advertisements for salespeople.

Figure 12 is a classic example of a totally self-centred advertisement. It talks at length about what *they* want and says nothing about what's in it for the applicant. It also has a box number, which means all the best people will totally ignore it, and all the second-best people will feel anxious in case it's their own company. All the useless people, however, will reply in droves.

Worse than that, by stating 'small' in line two, and then asking for 'salary details', this company is making it clear indeed that it is looking to pay the **lowest** salary it can get away with. The only saving grace in the advert is the main title -- Sales Executive -- which is second only to 'Manager' for turning people on.

Now let's look at the opposite of that (Figure 13) from a company which knows that it is selling, and makes a good job of it; a company which knows that when you go the trouble of exposing your company in an advertisement you might as well have a go at selling the product as well as finding the people you are looking for. Every bit of exposure is worth money, so don't waste any opportunities.

SALES EXECUTIVE

Required for their overseas division by small Birmingham based exhibition organisers. Applicants, m/f, must have proven ability to secure sales of exhibition space for specialist industrial events throughout the world. The ideal candidate will demonstrate convincing evidence of strong skills and determination to achieve success in a competitive environment.

Although first and foremost a sales appointment experience of other aspects of exhibition promotion and organisation will be valued.

Apply in strictest confidence with full career and salary details, to:
Box No. MFV 26

Figure 12

That is a great selling job. Right from the first subheading they are dangling carrots in front of the reader. They give the company's products a good write up, which can never hurt, and they tell the potential applicant just what he can expect to get from the job. They also make him feel important and sought after and they give him the opportunity to take instant action.

The only mistake which this company could make now would be for the manager whose name appears in the ad not to be answering his own phone for the next week or two.

If you take those initial calls personally, you will be saving yourself weeks of preliminary interviews, because you can do it all on the phone. That means you are immediately into the second and third interviews.

How to avoid the losers

If your business is to succeed you have to be able to pick winners and avoid losers. I have two pet systems for picking winners, both very

Figure 13

simple. If you are interviewing for a sales position, all the applicants will probably be clever enough to give you the answers you want to hear to the usual run of questions.

If I am looking for experienced people, then they have to prove that all their experience is worth something. So I challenge them to prove how good they are.

I say: 'Okay, show me the evidence of your last seven years in this business. Show me your 'well done' letters, the commission statements, the league tables, whatever you've got that proves to me you are what you say you are.'

If they can't show me anything because they've forgotten it, or never collected all the evidence in the first place, then they are off my list, because they are either fools or liars, and I don't want to hire either.

Alternatively I say to them: 'Tell me about yourself from day two of your life, the day after you popped out of your mother's womb. Just sketch over it, to give me an idea how you grew up.' It takes people off their guard. What I'm looking for is people who like being with other people. I'm trying to identify the loners who never join in on anything, but I don't look for the captain of the school cricket team unless I want a potential sales manager. I'm looking for 'indians' not 'chiefs', and I'm looking for people who 'enjoy' people, which is a characteristic which is formed in the first seven years of life.

In my experience you are either a 'people' person, or a loner, and it's the former which make the good salespeople. They are the ones who do business with people every day and who have to be liked by everyone they meet. For the loner that is very hard indeed.

These two methods will usually throw up four applicants out of thirty or forty who can prove a track record, and who are obviously the right sort of 'people' people.

Good feelings or hunches about people should be kept until the last interview. Feelings in your water that 'this guy is going to fit in', can lead you to hiring someone who you will be firing three months later. But if you have been through all the preliminaries, then you can feel safer about following your instincts, particularly if you are having difficulty deciding between the last two or three people.

In the first and second interviews you need to take all the emotion out of the job, and work to a formal system. You must work out in advance a detailed profile of the person you want, with all the specifications like age, location, marital status, financial situation, education, experience, motivation, aspirations and health all taken into consideration (see Figure 14).

You can then draw up three grades – perfect, average and no good, giving the interviewees marks between zero and four in each category. At the end of the interviews you simply tot up the totals and the highest scores are the people who should be seen again. This is an ideal checklist for a preliminary telephone interview.

So, provided you get the profile right in advance, it should all happen hunch-free.

Applicant's name Home address <div style="text-align:center">Phone</div>							S C O R E
Age	25 to 33	4	From 22 to 37	2	Under 22 or over 37	0	
Location	Bristol	4	Within 5 mile radius of Bristol	2	Outside 5 mile radius of Bristol	0	
Marital status	Married with children	4	Single or married with no children	2	Divorced or separated	0	
Financial situation	Assets and reasonable mortgage	4	No debts and no mortgage	2	No assets and debts	0	
Education	'O' levels or CSEs + further training	4	CSEs with no further training	2	No Qualifications	0	
Experience in selling	Well trained in selling	4	Some sales history	2	No sales history	0	
Experience in markets	Compre-hensive experience	4	Some experience	2	No experience	0	
Knowledge of products	Full knowledge	4	Some knowledge	2	No knowledge	0	
Motivation	Highly financially motivated	4	Status conscious	2	Wants car and freedom	0	
Aspirations	Keen to develop as a salesperson	4	Move into management	2	No views held	0	
Health	Extremely fit	4	Looks in good health	2	Weak and unfit	0	
					Total score		

Figure 14

The shortlist interview

My favourite recruitment technique is reserved for the final short listed candidates. I call it the 'Four for Dinner' technique. It is the only thing in recruitment which I have found to be 100 per cent infallible. It's also fun, and you and your spouse get a good dinner at the company's expense.

It is also deadly serious. It is the 'can't afford to make a mistake' business of positive vetting. The fun element is purely secondary. It is a technique which everyone who ever recruits salespeople and all senior executives should learn to use, and use well.

If you are proposing to give a successful candidate responsibility for the success or failure of part of your business, you must thoroughly check out your final candidates. It is only common-sense. You might hire a good private detective to do the job for you, but that way you will just end up with a report with no 'feel'.

So you and your spouse must invite the candidate and their spouse out to dinner. 'I always make a point of meeting the candidate's spouse,' you explain, 'and the evening time is usually more convenient, it certainly is for us.'

You suggest a restaurant near to the candidate's home and you **state** – not suggest – that you'll pick them both up **at their home**, on the agreed date at the agreed time.

When you drive up to collect them, you're **deliberately** ten minutes early, so that it's an odds-on bet you'll be invited in for a glass of something. If you're not, then he's lost three points on the social graces scale and your spouse will have to plead a weak bladder.

Now you get to see the *inside* of their home. You inspect the bookshelves – see what kind of books he reads – **and** the video. You suss out the animal kingdom, and quickly learn the rules of the roost – him, her, or the Rotweiler? You check out their 'Yuppy' status.

Find out about his attitude to tidiness by asking where he does his homework. Either he will show you, or his wife will tell you she doesn't allow him to!

Check out his car as well. What state is it in? Is that how you like your cars to look?

By the time you are driving to the restaurants, half your shortlist candidates will have eliminated themselves.

Once you are at the restaurant you let the candidate choose the wine (you're driving!). If he chooses the Piesporter or the Mateus Rosé, that's another three points gone.

You will really start to learn the truth when the candidate and his spouse start arguing amongst themselves. The objective is to get your guests mildly tiddled!. My wife and I have become experts at setting up arguments between candidate and spouse, and at times it really does 'all hang out'.

I have had a candidate get through to the Four for Dinner evening with ten out of ten, and then dive back to zero out of ten over the meal. His wife scored ten, and I would have offered her the job if she hadn't been married to **him**! I bet she didn't half kick him when they got back home.

If it's a question of picking winners and losers, you must be as sure as you can be. Don't think that this is going over the top, or that you've no right to invade people's privacy in this way, or to deliberately set them up – you have **every** right.

If your recruitment campaign doesn't give you the person you want – then do it all again. Don't accept second best or, to put it another way:

Never hire seconds

Keep this sign in front of you right through the recruitment procedure. If you ignore it, you'll become a second-rate business before you can blink.

Making job descriptions work

Everybody who works in the business world should have a job description, from managing director to messenger boy. Working without one is like trying to steer a ship without a compass – it will be impossible to travel in the right direction.

Most job descriptions are inadequate. They fail to achieve their objectives because they have been badly designed. As a result, people lose their way or cannot be held accountable when things go wrong.

The average job description contains four elements.

1   Purposes of the job.
2   Functions that have to be undertaken. And how.
3   Reporting up, down and sideways.
4   Relationships with other people in the organization.

There are, however, at least another three elements which most people omit:

5   *Authority:*   Authority is critical. What authority does this person have to hire, fire, negotiate, give discounts, spend money or commit the business in whatever way?
6   *Performance standards:*   In each element of the job description the standard of performance which is deemed acceptable must be defined. Without it the document is totally meaningless.
7   *Training and prospects*
     Standard of performance, training and prospects are the most important aspects of this mix because, and this requires another sign,

---

People need to grow

From day one you need to give people all the encouragement they need to grow, and point them in the right direction with visible signs of how they should be progressing.

In many companies the training and prospects aspects are covered in a separate document called a 'personnel development programme', which is probably attached to the job description rather than being integrated into it.

Figure 15 is an example of a job description which illustrates what can be done to define standards of performance. Use one like this in your recruitment interviews. The sooner you know how an applicant feels about your standards of performance the better.

SAMPLE JOB DESCRIPTION

JOB TITLE: Field Sales Representative

REPORTING TO: Field Sales Manager (FSM)
                    with liaison with other company departments as necessary.

MAIN RESPONSIBILITIES:

To be fully responsible for all company business in the territory from when an enquiry is solicited to the time that the company is paid in full.

Additionally:
   to meet and surpass the minimum objectives and standards of performance;
   to meet and surpass the targets set from time to time by the company;
   to plan to develop as an increasingly effective field salesperson.

Reproduced by kind permission of

Structured Training plc
Concorde House, 24 Warwick New Road, Royal Leamington Spa, Warwickshire CV32 5JH
Telephone: 0926 37621-6 Telex: 317488 Fax: 0926 311316

Figure 15

KEY TASKS:

1   ATTAINING SALES TARGETS AND OBJECTIVES

Standards of performance relating to the above are attained when:

a)   total sales volume and sterling value are in accordance with plan;
b)   product mix is in accordance with plan;
c)   total call rate does not fall below agreed minimum standard;
d)   the employee monitors own performance at least monthly, noting any deviation from plan, and suggesting remedial action to the FSM;
e)   personal objectives are set superior to those set by the company.

2   COVERING THE TERRITORY EFFECTIVELY

Standards of performance relating to the above are attained when:

a)   all existing accounts and prospects are graded by market type;
b)   calls are correctly balanced between existing accounts and prospects;
c)   actual itinerary does not deviate extensively from calling plan;
d)   calls are made on existing accounts according to potential thus:

GRADE:	POTENTIAL:	CALL FREQUENCY:
A	over 5,000 tonnes p.a.	every 2 weeks
B	3,000 – 5,000 tonnes p.a.	every 4 weeks
C	1,000 – 3,000 tonnes p.a.	every 6 weeks
D	under 1,000 tonnes p.a.	every 12 weeks

3   REPORTING ON ACTIVITIES AND CONFORMING TO ADMINISTRATION SYSTEMS

Standards of performance relating to the above are attained when:

a)   reports are neatly and accurately written;
b)   daily reports are posted to the FSM at the end of each working day;
c)   action reports are sent to the sales office, with a copy to the FSM;
d)   competition reports are sent to the FSM without delay;
e)   information on large potential contracts is sent to the sales office, and the FSM is notified of the details by telephone;
f)   a complaint form is completed whenever a claim is possible;
g)   expenses are submitted to the FSM at the end of each working week;
h)   sickness involving absence from work is reported to the FSM and to Personnel Department during the morning of the first day absent;
i)   holidays are agreed with the FSM at least 4 weeks in advance;
j)   estimates over £100 for motor repair are sent to the FSM for approval;
k)   any form of accident is reported to the FSM within 24 hours.

4   KEEPING ADEQUATE RECORDS

Standards of performance in relation to the above are attained when:

a)   customer record cards are neatly written and are always up to date;
b)   record cards are consulted before each call to plan sales tactics;

5   UNDERSTANDING FULLY THE PRODUCTS AND SERVICES OF THE COMPANY

Standards of performance in relation to the above are attained when:

a)   the full range of products and services are thoroughly understood;
b)   there is confidence in the ability to present each product skilfully;
c)   when customer queries can be answered quickly and confidently.
d)   there is regular analysis to ensure that the full range is offered;

6   MAKING THE MAXIMUM CONVERSION OF TIME

Standards of performance in relation to the above are attained when:

a)   a diary is used skilfully;
b)   the amount of face-to-face selling time is optimised;
c)   departure from home in the morning is not later than 8.30 am.;
d)   the first customer call is made not later than 9.15 am.;
e)   departure from the last customer call is not earlier than 4.30 pm.;
f)   the average duration of a customer call is limited to 30 minutes;
g)   good route planning reduces the amount of driving time to a minimum.

7   HAVING FULL MARKET KNOWLEDGE OF THE SALES AREA

Standards of performance in relation to the above are attained when there is full knowledge of:

a)   all the outlets in the area for the company products and services;
b)   the potential of these outlets by product and service;
c)   all decision makers and influencers at the customer locations;
d)   major future contracts and tenders likely to come from the area;
e)   all competitors working on the area and their market shares;
f)   competitors' personnel, products and services, and business methods.

8   KEEPING COMPANY COSTS TO A MINIMUM

Standards of performance in relation to the above are attained when:

a)   selling costs are kept to a minimum – and certainly within budget;
b)   the most profitable way is sought to take orders for the company;
c)   customer service is carried out effectively to minimise claims;
d)   all intelligence on customers' credit worthiness is passed to the FSM;
e)   there is full awareness of the state of customers' accounts;
f)   there is liaison with company Credit Control on outstanding accounts;
g)   all company property is carefully handled and well maintained.

9   SELF DEVELOPMENT

Standards of performance in relation to the above are attained when:

a)   product presentation is frequently practised alone and with others;
b)   a continuous programme is carried out of reading and other study on salesmanship and subjects related to company products and services;
c)   medium and long term objectives are set in relation to the job, and these are regularly discussed and assessed with the FSM.

Training and development

The right approach to this subject is summed up in that well-known biblical saying:

Give a man a fish and you feed him for a day
Teach him to fish and you feed him for life.

If you ignore training and development you will always lose your best people, and you will end up spending five times as much money on recruitment as you need to. It is always better to hang on to the good people you have got, hopefully making them better all the time, than taking the chance of being able to replace them with other good people when they go. Even if you are lucky and do replace them, there will always be an interruption to the flow of business, and an expensive 'learning curve' as the new person finds his feet.

Training is not like an injection, however, one jab and you're cured. It is a continuous process to maintain good business health, and needs to be matched as closely as possible to the specific, identified needs of the individuals concerned. This is why outside training resources are so critical to most companies, because you can only really provide general training courses in-house. If you want to help one individual employee with the specific problems he faces in his job, you have to find the most appropriate course or seminar from amongst the many on offer to businesses from the major providers of training services.

Avoid one-man-bands. They are cheaper on fees, but only strong on native wit, not in-depth, up-to-date experience. It's the old 'monkeys for peanuts' situation.

Service contracts

Too many companies don't bother to give their people adequate service contracts, only the bare statutory minimum. They believe anything else is pointless because they will never be able to make restrictive covenants and restraint clauses stick. If you get it right, however, you can make them stick. You are basically aiming to protect yourself from competition from the people who work for you. Over the years you will have made them privy to your secrets and your techniques. You have to take precautions to stop them from taking that knowledge and setting up in direct competition. You have both the legal and moral right to protect yourself.

A restraint clause has to fit a number of clearly defined criteria if it is to work. First, the timescale should not be more than two years. Anything more than that you will have difficulty enforcing. Second, you must specify the geographical area within which the person actually worked, and thus must not set up a rival business. Once defined, you will then have to stick to it. Third, you must also define the company, division, products and services which the individual was directly concerned with, because they are the only things you will be able to enforce. If you have the time, geography and business definitions clearly laid out, you will be able to protect yourself.

You also have every right to demand confidentiality from your people regarding the secrets of your company and business, and there is a lot of flexibility available on the protection of inventions.

If somebody is working for you full time, you generally have the ownership of anything which they might invent while with you, but you should define this in the service contract.

You can insist that company property like cars are returned. There is a little known common law rule which states that if one of your people has a company car and you decide to fire that person, offering salary in lieu of notice in order to get rid of them quickly, then that person is entitled to the continuing use of the company car for the period during which he should have served out his notice.

To get the car back early, you will have to pay out an additional sum in order to allow the person to purchase a comparable car during the same period. You are not, however, liable for the running costs of the vehicle.

If you want to avoid this situation, you must insert a clause into the service contract which states that the company has a prior claim on the car if there is a priority need for it.

No surprises

You need to table the draft contract of employment, company car rules etc. during the *second interview*.

Moonlighters and leadswingers

Moonlighters are the folks who have second jobs. At their most romantic they play in jazz bands until four in the morning, at the more mundane level they are freelance reps for some new wonder product which pays commission only. On the other hand their wives may own fish and chip shops which they help with, or mobile catering businesses or whatever.

The law says that the employer cannot restrict an employee's activities outside the working hours for which you pay him. What happens, however, if someone who you have entrusted with a high-powered job is not working at his best because of other commitments? Do you really want to hire people who will only have the company interests at heart between nine and five?

You could put something in the service contract to the effect that this is not a nine to five job, and that a certain degree of flexibility is required. You could also build in a paragraph which says that you expect the person you are employing to be physically and mentally fit to do the work he is paid for. If he rolls up in the morning, bleary eyed and half asleep, he is not going to be able to do his job justice. You will then have every right to find out what is making him tired, and request that he stop it. Because they have the law on their side, however, you have to be sure that you approach it in the right way.

Leadswingers are the dishonest ones who are actually not doing the things which they tell you they are. They are the ones who file reports that say they made seventeen calls that day, when you know they only made two because they were off painting their house or taking the kids to the zoo.

Once a manager suspects someone of leadswinging, it can develop into an obsession, with tiny molehills growing into gigantic mountains. The answer is to take fast action, and hire a private detective. Get that person followed for a week — if the report turns out to be negative then you will have a great weight lifted off your mind. If it's positive then give it to the person in question to read, and then hand them a final letter of warning and tell them you don't expect them to do it again.

You will then have to do the odd random check if his figures don't seem to be up to scratch, and if you catch him again you can dismiss him on the spot, with a memo to the rest of the team, telling them what you have done and why. That way you gain the respect of the rest of them, and no-one else is likely to try to get one over on you for at least a few months.

Many managers would not dream of doing something like this. It may not sound pleasant but it is quick, effective and practical – and there is no alternative which won't drag on for months and lose the company a lot of money.

Filling sudden holes

When a sudden hole appears due to a sacking or an unexpected resignation or death, don't be too quick to fill it.

The chances are that you have got too many people on the payroll anyway, with all of them working at about 20 per cent of their full potential. All of you are probably spending too much time worrying about, and discussing, other people's problems rather than doing the job you are paid for.

If you suddenly lose somebody, take the opportunity to reorganize. The management 'laws' laid down by C. Northcote Parkinson in 1958, still hold true today:

- Work expands so as to fill the time available for its completion.
- It's the busiest man who has time to spare.
- Executives seek to multiply subordinates, not rivals.
- Executives make work for each other.

So bear in mind that you have too many people, and you don't need them all. The leaner you are the fitter you are.

It's no good just slimming down during the bad times and then fattening up again when things get easier. The good times will never last forever, so you need to remain in control, and keep your operation tight all the time, so that you are ready for the problems when they arrive.

Robert Townsend also had a quote to cover this in *Further Up the Organization*:* 'To keep an organisation young and fit, don't hire anyone until everyone is so overworked they will be glad to see the newcomer, no matter where he sits.'

There are, of course, exceptions to this rule, and some holes do have to be filled fast. A good manager should therefore keep a file of possible

* Michael Joseph, 1984

replacements for all the key people should the worst happen. The file could be built up from little snippets of gossip gleaned from meetings, letters and telephone calls. Even the competition might give you some ideas, or you may hear of people currently working in other industries.

Keep all the information in a dossier, so that if you have a sudden hole you do at least have a starting point. It will cut down your recruitment spending enormously if it proves successful.

Have you, for instance, looked at your service engineers recently? Some of them might make great salespeople. If you are aware of them and their abilities, you can be getting them involved and helping them to grow in their jobs.

You should be training successors for all your key people – that way you should never have a sudden hole for more than a few weeks – just long enough for the new person to fit in. This is true right to the top of the company. If the big boss has a heart attack tomorrow, do you have any idea who will fill his shoes?

It might also be worth considering 'key man insurance', whereby the company insures the most important people in the business, so that should one of them fall under a bus, the company receives enough money to tide them over until a replacement can be found.

Pruning for strength

The importance of pruning is now more widely accepted in most businesses, but it is never an easy thing to do. Peter Drucker, the world-famous management author, laid out the objectives for pruning in his book *Managing in Turbulent Times**: 'Concentrate resources on results. Feed the opportunities. Starve the problems.' That's not just the people, that's the business, the projects. Concentrate resources on results.

He also suggested setting some goals: 'We need to double the productivity of money in the business within eight to ten years. We need to produce 50 per cent more output within eight to ten years without increasing the number of people employed.' Both these goals are obtainable, but both require hard work. Only after they have been achieved do you have true growth.

It is you, however, who has to decide who to prune. If you want to prune for strength, see who fits these three criteria, which we can put

* Heinemann 1980

in the form of signs, at least one of which will already be familiar to you:

> **Is what I am doing or about to do getting us closer to our objective of making us money?**
> *(Robert Townsend)*

Look for the people in your organization who are spending most of their time doing things that do not contribute to either of those objectives, they must be suspect:

> **If you're not part of the solution, you've got to be part of the problem**

If you just think about that one for a few minutes you will be able to see who it applies to in your business:

> **If you have a guy who's good in a crisis, get rid of him, or you'll always have one**
> *(Robert Townsend)*

Interdepartmental relationships

There is another sign which sums up the feelings which we all have about our workmates at some time or another:

> **It's difficult to soar with eagles when you work with turkeys**

Many of you will be fortunate enough to be part of interdepartmental meetings, where the heads of all the departments get together to see what the rest are up to. Before the next meeting, try sending round a memo to all your colleagues who will be at the meeting, with a checklist attached. The checklist could contain any number of different questions such as: 'In relation to other departments, which of the following are causing delays or problems in my department, and should be discussed at management meetings?':

- Relevant information not being transmitted to other departments.
- Incomplete information received from other departments.
- Work flow interruptions caused by constant requests for immediate action or information.
- Formal lines of communication being ignored or bypassed.
- Verbal communications lacking in clarity, resulting in misunderstandings and misinterpretations.
- Requests for action or information not complied with.
- A build-up of frustration caused by poor communications between departments.

You then give them some columns to tick, headed 'not applicable', 'yes', 'no', 'action'.

Other questions might include: 'Is any one person or department consistently lacking in good communication? Are we inclined to rely too heavily on verbal communication? Are documents date-stamped by departments to show dates of receipt and completion? Are documents coded to indicate the degree of priority? Is the principle of "Do it now" sufficiently instilled in managers and staff?'

By the time you all get into the meeting, discussion will be raging – and I mean raging – and you will have to take your fair share of the flack for half an hour or so. At the end of that time, however, ask everyone just to sit quietly for a moment and reflect on everything that has just happened, and learn from it. I guarantee that from then on your meetings will get better and better, because the air has been cleared and everyone has been given a chance to come clean and air his grievances.

Body language

It helps a great deal if you can acquire some of the skills of reading body language. It will help you see what other people are thinking and not saying.

Let me give you some short examples of how it can work.

Boredom is usually pretty easy to spot in someone else (Figure 16) and you need to ask yourself why you are boring this person.

Figure 16

Figure 17

Figure 18

Figure 19

Figure 20

But what seems like simple boredom might be something more complex. What if the person sitting opposite you is fluttering his fingers over his lips as in Figure 17? Could it be that he wants to say something, rather than that he is trying to stifle a yawn? Perhaps you should invite him to speak. If you don't give him a chance to let it out, the thought might be lost forever.

What about the man who is obviously not happy? He is rubbing his nose with his knuckles, frowning with his chin down – easy to spot if you are watching (Figure 18).

Then there is the stiff, nervous, uncomfortable look, with clenched fists grasping at the trousers above the knees (Figure 19). Why is he feeling so bad in your company? If you are disciplining him, you are not doing it very well. If you are going to fire him, you had better get on with it.

There is also the classic angry look, rejecting whatever you are suggesting with arms tightly folded, ankles crossed, jacket buttoned, chin down, mouth corners down and a frown. He is defensive (Figure 20).

You must be aware of all these signs, and work to change them, and therefore the attitudes which they illustrate. When the chin comes up

Figure 21

or the arms unfold, or the head goes on one side, you know that you are beginning to get through.

The pyramided hands in Figure 21 are not exactly a rejection, but they are critical. If you can bring those hands down across the stomach in a clasp rather than a fold, you are getting somewhere. If the person then leans forward, opening up with the hands still clasped you have a complete, happy, positive reception. That is when you strike the deal, closing the sale or whatever your objective is.

The postmortem

We've all experienced the meetings which are held to find out why something has gone wrong. If they are to be useful they must be got together fast, with the aim of putting the problem right.

It is vital, therefore, that they are constructive and not destructive. Hatchet meetings are out. If your personal style is going to make it seem like a hatchet meeting, and you can't change your style, then you will have to let someone else handle it, otherwise everyone will clam up and you will achieve nothing.

Checklist

1   Treat recruitment as a selling exercise.
2   Learn to pick winners and avoid losers.
3   Create workable job descriptions.
4   Create good training and development programmes.
5   Always draw up service contracts which include restraint clauses.
6   Deal firmly with moonlighters and leadswingers.
7   Plan for future staff changes.
8   Prune for strength.
9   Rethink your relationships with other departments.
10   Learn to read body language.

8

Communications

Do you communicate with your people mainly formally or informally? The formal route takes you through written memos and reports to organized meetings. The informal starts with bumping into people in the corridor, and probably ends at lunch over a drink in the local bar.

Both methods have their advantages and disadvantages, and the ideal is to have a judicious mix of the two.

The grapevine

If you have two or more people gathered together, the grapevine will always be there, so there's no point in letting it aggravate you. What you must do is make sure that it is working to your advantage. Which means that you must actively use it.

What it does is fuel speculation. If you put in the right information you can use it to change opinions and attitudes, or to generate interest in a new idea.

As well as putting information into the grapevine, you must also listen to what comes out. If things are going wrong anywhere in the company the grapevine will be the first thing to give you some intimation of the problems. It can act as a storm warning, telling you of clouds massing beyond your own horizon.

Managers are often surprised to find that grapevines know what decisions they are going to make before they make them. Office gossip will often know who you are going to fire or promote before you even know yourself.

The briefing group

Managers should insist that all supervisors should hold small weekly meetings with their immediate groups of people. They should only consist of three or four people, and they only need to last for fifteen or twenty minutes.

During the meeting they can mull over what has happened in the previous week: What are they pleased about? What went well? What went badly? What will happen next week? What's the workload like? Are they winning new bits and pieces of business? Have they got a heavy load of paperwork? What's the company doing? What should they prepare themselves for? What are other departments doing?

It has to be a regular weekly discipline, insisted upon by management, who will provide the people with something to input.

From time to time the manager should also attend the briefing, not to take over but to sit on the sidelines, watching and answering any questions which they might have. The briefing must always, however, be run by the supervisor.

By attending the meeting the manager will get a feedback on what his people are thinking about, what is worrying them and what problems they have got.

Managers should also be running the same sorts of briefings with their own immediate sets of supervisors.

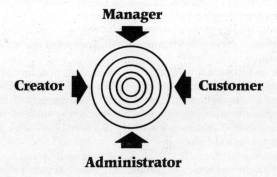

Figure 22

Quality circles

The quality circle originated in Japan, and is normally associated with a particular product like a car or a camera. The idea is to find better ways to make whatever the product is. The theory works just as well in any sphere of business, and all managers should use it.

You start by putting together a group of four or five people and giving them the task of looking at the quality of what you do as a company. How well do you work? How well do you satisfy your customers? How well do you do your part of the job? How can you improve it? There are no limits to what they can discuss.

The group receives its information from all the furthest areas of the business, from the managers, the customers, the administrators and the actual creators of the product or providers of the service. They will hear everyone's views, complaints and problems and will discuss them (Figure 22).

You then print them up some special headed paper, upon which they can jot down all their suggestions, ideas or conclusions, and circulate them around the managers. The managers can then take action on what has been discussed. Insist that they come up with at least one idea a month on how you can improve the quality of what you do. You will be amazed at the difference you can make over a working year.

Noticeboards and house magazines

In many companies noticeboards and house magazines are left either to the personnel department or the public relations people. Everyone else seems to find them an enormous bore. This is a mistake and every manager should make it his business to find out what is happening in both these areas.

There is a format for noticeboards, which no one should ignore (Figure 23). Standing instructions should be off to the left, Priority items should be at the top right, with social items at the bottom right. All the routine business can then be fitted into the spaces left in the middle. You should also have a brightly coloured arrow which points to the latest item to be stuck up.

The trouble with noticeboards is that people rush up and down past them, and might not notice that something new has gone up.

If you have a board, you must keep it up to date. Nothing gives a

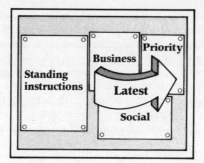

Figure 23

visitor to a company a worse impression than some notice which looks as if it has been dipped in coffee, hanging on one pin and announcing the Christmas party of the previous year.

To avoid this you must make one person responsible – possibly your right-hand lady – and she must ensure that the moment a notice is no longer relevant, it is removed. The staff will soon realize that anything which remains pinned up is relevant, and will take the trouble to read it.

. House magazine editors often get a very raw deal from managers who can't be bothered to come up with good, positive, useful information about what they and their teams are up to. Never believe that you are too busy to be bothered with such trivia. Make it a rule to provide at least one really interesting story for each issue. It could be Mary having a baby, Charlie getting a promotion, or the winning of a major new contract. It doesn't matter, as long as it's there.

It is always better if a story can be accompanied with photographs. They can be black and white and they don't have to be taken by a professional. It costs very little to shoot a couple of pictures of a contract signing, or the unveiling of a new piece of machinery, or a send-off party for Fred's retirement, but it will make all the difference to the morale of your team when they frequently see themselves in print.

Personal presentation

Senior managers are often the worst at personal presentation in the company, possibly because nobody has dared to tell them how dull they are. We have all been to the sales conference where everything was swinging along until the top brass stood up and began droning on. Everyone then begins to shuffle their feet if it is before lunch, or drop off if it's after lunch, and nothing has been achieved by anyone.

Effective managers must learn the skills of personal communications – and they really aren't hard – if they hope to put across points of company policy or to communicate their plans for the future.

You don't have to be born a great speaker, you just have to acquire the right skills. You start by studying the rules and then practise as much as possible. It's not hard to persuade people to let you speak, because no one else ever wants to do it. There are lots of occasions like retirement presentations, and toasts at formal dinners. The first rule is to volunteer for everything, even when your first instinct is to get out of it as quickly as possible.

If you have had plenty of practice on these small jobs, you should have no trouble when the 'big one' comes along.

The second rule is not to worry about all the things that other people worry about. You will get attacks of nerves, it is inevitable, so you will have to accept them. With no nervous tension your presentation will be completely flat.

Fear of the unknown is the next great stumbling block, so get to know the venue in advance. Don't be one of those speakers who turns up five minutes before he's due on stage, and then can't work the equipment or even find the right room. Get there when nobody is around and walk about to see where you are going to be and familiarize yourself with the surroundings.

Many of us are also scared of ourselves, in case we forget our words, trip over the wires, or foam at the mouth. In reality most of us do none of these things, and if we do then no-one in the audience even notices. So unless there is a record of insanity in the family, don't worry about how you will react under the lights.

Speakers are often frightened of their audiences, which is illogical since you can nearly always escape off the stage faster than they can get onto it. Seriously, most audiences are very sympathetic to speakers, as long as they don't bore them or do anything silly, usually because they are very grateful that it isn't them up there.

You might also be afraid of being misunderstood. That could be a very real problem, but it is one which is easily overcome. You simply have to ensure that your message is so clearly thought out that there is no room left for misunderstanding.

Fear of not being heard is also very real. If the meeting is large enough you will have microphones and all the necessary back-up. If not then you will have to rely on your own voice projection. That will require practice. The real secret is always but always to talk to the back row, not the front row.

Try holding meetings in larger rooms, and ask you colleagues to help. When you are in a meeting tell them what you are doing, and then talk to them from the far end of the room, asking them to inform you if there's anything they can't hear. Practice is the only way to improve your projection.

Stage fright is very real, although I have never yet seen anyone who is struck completely dumb by it. Everyone seems to get by somehow. To help build your own self-confidence, however, make sure that you know the first sixty seconds of your speech absolutely off by heart. Once you have got through that first minute, you will find that the rest will flow out surprisingly naturally.

Write your own notes. Never, never get someone else to type them and then try to read the typed script. Write them yourself in letters large enough for you to read three or four feet away. Use different colours to highlight key points, and avoid joined-up writing.

One last tip – leave the jokes to the comedians! Telling jokes is one of the hardest jobs in the world, and completely different from being a communicator. Stick to your job and leave the comedy to the people who are paid for it.

Visual aids

Visual aids are important for any communication. They provide texture to the information you are presenting, and they will improve recall amongst the audience.

Percentage recall of information				
Method of conveying information	3 hours later (%)	3 days later (%)	3 weeks later (%)	3 months later (%)
Telling and showing together	85	65	28	16
Showing (just pictures)	72	20	12	7
Telling (just voice)	70	10	7	3

Figure 24

Figure 24 demonstrates very dramatically how visual aids will help. It shows that if you are a very exceptional speaker, using no aids at all, you might get 70 per cent recall from your audience after three hours, but from then on it will start to disappear. You would do better if you just showed them the pictures. But if you combine the two together, recall improves signficantly.

Having decided that visual aids are vital to any speaker, you then have to decide what sort of aids to use, and how to employ them. The range available on the market is enormous, from felt pens and flip charts up to the most sophisticated computer graphics and video techniques.

If you are in any doubt, always opt for simplicity. The worst than can happen with a flip chart is that your pen dries up or the stand falls over. Finding another pen isn't hard, and you can always pick the stand up again in a few seconds. With high technology there is no end to the variety of problems which can arise, from exploding bulbs to loose plugs and faulty microchips.

Simplicity also adds to your flexibility. If you have a fixed slide presentation, your words have to remain synchronized. If you are running out of time, or feel the attention of your audience slipping away, there is nothing you can do about it, you have to stick to your original script.

There is no question, that, if it works well, a good slide presentation will make you look very professional, but it is worth weighing up the potential problems – and costs – when you make your initial decisions on how to present.

Checklist

1   Use the grapevine constructively.
2   Set up briefing groups.
3   Set up quality circles.
4   Use noticeboards and house magazines.
5   Learn the skills of personal presentation.
6   Always use visual aids.

9
Management Techniques

If you ask managers what their real job is, you will usually receive answers like: 'I run the transport,' or 'I am in charge of sales.' That is a description of their work, but not really of their jobs.

Any manager's job is to make a contribution to the performance of the business. That doesn't necessarily mean 'doing things', which is what most of us do in the jobs we hold before becoming managers. It is very hard to change from 'doing things' to 'managing things'.

If they aren't careful, managers can become passengers in the company, merely processing the work instead of making a management contribution.

As you go through the day, ask yourself at each stage: 'Is this a management function? Am I exercising my talents as a manager or am I *doing* something? If I am just doing something, is it something which I could give to someone else to do? Instead of filling in these forms myself, could my right-hand person do it, if I showed her how? Could someone else be drawing these office layouts while I *manage* something instead?'

Managing or doing – a ten-minute test

Which of the following activities would you say were managing as distinct from non-managing (or doing) activities?

1 Calling on an account with one of your salespeople to show a customer that the company management is interested in the account.
2 Making a sales presentation to a prospective customer in order to show one of your salespeople how to do it.

3   Making an independent call on a senior manager of a large account in order to cement customer relationships and promote business.

4   Explaining how to solve a work problem which one of your people has just brought to you.

5   Filling out a form to recommend a salary increase for a member of your department.

6   Interviewing a prospective salesperson referred to you by an employment agency.

7   Asking one of your salespeople what he thinks about a selling idea you have had.

8   Planning and deciding on objectives for future sales volume by account.

9   Deciding what the cost budget request should be for your sales office.

10   Reviewing monthly sales reports to determine progress towards specific sales objectives.

11   Deciding whether to recommend adding an additional staff member in a new position.

12   Designing an improved layout for the sales office.

13   Asking your salespeople to establish tentative six-month objectives for the number of personal sales calls to be made on target accounts.

14   Transferring an account from Salesperson A to Salesperson B because Salesperson A did not devote the necessary effort to developing that account.

15   Planning the extent to which your salespeople should use staff services during the next year to accomplish overall sales objectives.

Turn to page 133 for the answers.

The 80/20 law

The 80/20 law says that you will spend 80 per cent of your time on things which achieve 20 per cent of the job. This law is invaluable and as a manager you will need to bear it in mind all the time if you are to avoid the booby traps of inefficient management.

You must question all your priorities and put them into the 'must, should and could' categories. Carry a notepad around with you, with those three words written on it. When you write yourself notes during the day, make sure they go under the right headings.

A **must** is an important task which contributes directly to your objectives, it is not something which would be nice to do if you can get round to it. Not only will the right priorities make you a more effective manager, they will also help to boost your career and your income.

Hunch, munch and punch

The hunch munch and punch approach to problem solving is to be avoided at all costs. The **hunch** means having a bright idea and acting on it without further thought, the **munch** is when you decide to 'chew it over', and keep on chewing while the problem grows bigger, and the **punch** is when you drown a problem in resources.

If you deluge a problem with resources you may well get rid of it, but you will almost certainly waste a lot of money at the same time.

Always use a team approach to problem solving, because several heads are always better than one, and then try to think laterally in order to get away from the conventional methods of problem solving. Ask yourself: 'What other ways could I solve this problem, apart from the obvious?'.

You will also fail to solve a problem if you don't allocate enough resources. You may quieten it down for a while, but it will undoubtedly be back. The good manager must be able to balance the cure with the need.

Decision making

> **The best managers are the ones who make the best decisions**

That sign is important enough to be engraved on all our hearts, because making and deferring decisions is one of the hardest management skills to learn.

Any decision is better than none, the tortoise may only make slow progress through life, but he makes none at all until he sticks his neck out.

Any salesperson will know that 80 per cent of people are bad decision makers, which is why salespeople have to learn how to help them make decisions, and sometimes to take the decisions for them. If you agree that salespeople should sell to decision makers, not to decision influencers, it follows that 80 per cent of managers are bad decision makers.

You need to use a decision-making format, which comes in three stages. First, when somebody comes to you for a decision, clarify it and query it, to ensure that they are actually asking for the right one under the circumstances.

You will then need to question the timing and the risk or cost involved. Say it is a simple decision, like what colour you are going to paint the bicycle sheds. A lot of people might agonize for ages over the problem, but if you weigh up the risks if you make a wrong decision (say £50 to repaint it another colour), you will see that it isn't worth spending time worrying about it. It is more cost-effective to make a fast decision and take the risk.

If, on the other hand, it is a fundamental decision like: 'What am I going to do with the company, and where are we going in the future?' then the risks are very high that if you make a bad decision you will ruin everything. That warrants a completely different level of decision making to the bicycle shed – but you would be amazed how many managers don't know how to differentiate between the two types of decision.

You must then combine hard research with your own experience, to work out what the critical elements in the problem are – there are always critical elements. They might be people, money or market movement. Once you have seen what is critical you can make your choice, implement and then monitor it.

Brainstorming

Brainstorming, by which I mean the deliberate generation of creative ideas, is a great way of obtaining the right input.

A few people will think creatively all the time. The majority, however, need to be pushed into it.

So, get together a group of no more than five people from mixed backgrounds, and outline the problem to them. You then say: 'Let's have any idea you like that will solve the problem.'

You must have a flip chart on which to record all the suggestions as they come out. When you reach the end of a page, don't turn it over, tear it out instead, and pin it on the wall so that everyone can see where you have got to so far.

You must recognize that no idea is stupid. Never put anybody down. Don't say: 'That's ridiculous,' or 'We couldn't do that!' There is no such thing as a stupid idea, because each one can lead on to another. The first may be impractical, but the one it leads on to may be perfect. Encourage the flow of all sorts of ideas.

You must teach the brainstormers to overcome their inhibitions. That means they musn't be frightened of saying something stupid or wrong. It takes time to train people to make their minds wander sideways, and then to have the confidence to voice the ideas which result from the wanderings. If you do it right, brainstorming will produce solutions to problems which you would never ever come up with for yourself.

Coordination

The main reason why projects come adrift once they have been conceived, is lack of coordination. You must define and limit what you are going to do, and then determine exactly who is responsible for what parts of it.

You must be able to communicate exactly what is to be done and why. There are five stages in coordinating a project:

- Information
- Intention
- Method
- Administration
- Intercommunication

Even on a simple project, say a prestige mailing to top customers and prospects, you must give the people involved all the background **information**. You must explain: 'We have been losing ground in this particular market and we think that one way of overcoming that is to send out a top-of-the-market mailing.'

Then you come to the **intention**: 'This mailing will go out weekly in

September and October, so many a week.' Next the **method**, which will cover what you will print up, who you will send it to, and **administration** which covers who does what to make the whole thing happen.

Finally you have **intercommunication**, which means deciding how the various members of the team will work together and ensuring everyone is going in the same direction.

If the people involved in the project don't have a total picture of the background, they might make a local decision which will wreck the whole project, simply because they don't understand the significance of what they are doing.

If, for instance, they ran out of white envelopes half way through the mailing, and had plenty of manilla ones in stock, someone who didn't know how important it was that the mailing looked superb might make a decision, based on speed and cost, to use the second-rate envelopes, thus undermining the whole project with a decision that was based on good sense at a local level.

Network analysis

It may sound rather a frightening term, but network analysis can be a very handy management tool. To illustrate how it works, let's take the simple example of building a house.

There is a long list of stages involved in the project – issue instructions, order materials, dig foundations, lay concrete, build walls, install roof trusses and tile the roof (Figure 25).

Many managers might try to work through the project with a list like that, allocating a certain number of days to each stage.

Building a House
Sequential Path

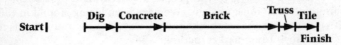

Figure 25

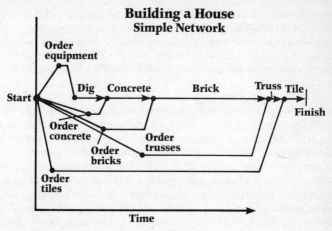

Figure 26

With network analysis you would look at all these stages and decide which ones had to be done in a certain order (you can't do the roof until the walls are up, for instance).

You will see that there is also a time base for each stage. What Figure 26 tells you is exactly by when you will have to have certain materials ordered and what the 'critical path' is.

The critical path in any project determines the overall length of the project. In the case of building the house the roof takes the longest because of the length of time if takes to order tiles. So by doing this analysis you can see that you need to order the tiles right at the beginning, whereas the man with the simple list might have left that until the end, being unable to spot the critical paths.

As soon as you lay the whole project out graphically you are able to pick out the sequential items, and can see at once which is the one critical item which is going to hold up the whole programme.

Taking on a new team

Taking on a new team is always a challenge, whether it is as a result of internal promotion or a move to a new company. Your first problem will be that the management from whom you are taking over will take their team for granted.

Everybody in your new department knows how it works, except you, and unless you insist on some sort of induction they may not bother to tell you anything. Every manager needs a decent induction to a new job.

You must then go into the department in a cautious and exploratory way. Unless it is a complete disaster don't change anything right away. Just sit tight and watch the way they do things, because they are the ones with experience and there may be very good reasons for everything they do. You will also be able to spot where the big problems are, rather than being distracted by a lot of day-to-day trivia.

If you rush in and change everything you will worry everyone, so stand back, ask questions, watch and listen. Talk to everyone, saying; 'You've worked here a long time, you must have ideas on how things could be improved. How can we make things quicker, easier, cheaper or more profitable?'

Most people have an awful lot of ideas, it's just that they never get a chance to express them, but watch out for people who might be trying to use you to settle old scores.

On a very practical level, when you take on the new job, go and buy yourself a brand new A4, lined, bound book. Carry it with you wherever you go and write everything down in it, all your ideas, all the ideas which other people give you and your assessment to those people. It will be an invaluable tool that you will use in the future transformation of the department.

If you hang on to the book, and refer to it continually, you won't lose track of the little things which you spotted when you first arrived, but which soon became submerged beneath the big things, and it will give you a plan to work to for the first six or twelve months.

At the end of that period you will be able to look through the book and see exactly how many of the ideas you have actually been able to put into force. If you don't record your impressions when you are a newcomer, you will soon lose that fresh perspective and start taking things for granted like everyone else.

Show your team that you are the sort of person who gets things done, and that changes will be for the better. If there aren't enough towels in the lavatories or the tea is disgusting, then do something about it, because these are the sorts of things which people notice and talk about. It will give them confidence in the future. You can move around some desks, or even knock down a wall, but make some physical gesture on things you are absolutely sure about, which shows that things are going to change.

Good housekeeping

You can tell a great deal about any company by the standards of their housekeeping. You can see as soon as you walk into a factory or office, just by looking around, and it hasn't got anything to do with money.

The way in which a place is looked after is a reflection of the attitude of the people who work there. You don't have to spend a fortune on the most expensive office systems, you just need to look after whatever you've got. Are the desks tidy for instance, or are there piles of paper all over the place?

Tomorrow morning try looking at your own place of work as if for the first time. Imagine what a first-time visitor would make of what he saw. If it looks tacky then he will assume you have tacky working habits, and it is your job as manager to put that impression right.

You must start by giving people the right facilities. If the only place available for the paper is the floor then that's where they will put it, so maybe they need shelves or filing systems or binders.

You must set an example with your own desk. If you go home leaving papers all over it, everyone else will do the same, and the next morning the place will look a mess when everyone gets in. Good housekeeping is something which you have to work at every day. But it will pay significant dividends in improved working habits. You also stop losing documents and eradicate situations where somebody takes two weeks to answer a letter because it got lost behind something else.

Negotiation

Every manager needs to know how to negotiate, both with his own people and with customers. It is a subject which merits a book all of its own (and there are several on the market).

Start by always using the 'negotiating zip' shown in Figure 27.

In any negotiation you need to be able to move from a position of agreement to a position of future agreement. Inexperienced negotiators tend to begin by thinking: 'Well now, the biggest problem we've

The Negotiating Zip

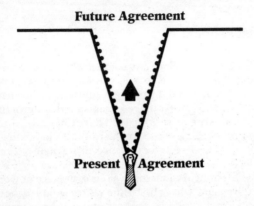

Figure 27

got to agree on is this. If we can agree on that, the rest is easy.' So they begin the negotiation by saying: 'Well George, the biggest problem we have got to look at is this, so that's where we'll start.' That is a fundamental error.

Supposing, instead of starting with the biggest area of disagreement, you started with an area of agreement, then you can say: 'Right, we've got a variety of things to discuss, and I believe that we both agree that . . . .' There must be something that you can agree on, even if it is only the need for a negotiation. 'There seem to be a lot of differences between us but obviously you agree with me that it's worthwhile sitting down and trying to negotiate some agreement over this, isn't it?' At which point the other guy says 'Yes', and every salesperson knows that if you can start with a yes you are moving in the right direction.

You then continue along the zip, taking each item in ascending order of difficulty. What you are doing is teaching the other person how to work with you, showing that you can reach agreement on things. He learns that you do give concessions, but that sometimes he has to do the same. By the time you reach the most difficult problem at the top of the zip the situation is completely different, because the other person has spent all this time agreeing with you, while learning how to negotiate with you. If you have agreed ten other things with him, he will feel much more inclined to agree the eleventh, and hardest thing, than if you had produced it right at the beginning.

Striking a better deal

Once you have reached an agreement, you should then see if you can find ways of improving the deal for both sides. Supposing he's agreed to buy eighty tons of your product the month after next. It would help you if he would order 100 tons, because that's a truckload, and it would help you if you could deliver a month early because you have a slack month coming up. That gives you two financial inducements which you can offer him.

The important thing is that the improvements have got to work for both sides, and the same goes for concessions. You should never just give them away, always trade one concession for another. So you always say to somebody: 'If you will do that, I can do that.' If he offers to give you a concession for nothing, of course, then you just take it and keep quiet. It means he's never done a course on negotiating.

There has to be a better way

I would like to end this chapter with that sign, which can apply to every part of your business operation – take no notice of the cynical ones amongst us who would add 'to earn a living'.

Checklist

1 Concentrate on 'managing' not 'doing'.

2 Learn to make decisions.

3 Use brainstorming sessions.

4 Make sure all your people coordinate their efforts.

5 Use network analysis.

6 Improve the housekeeping of the whole department.

7 Learn to negotiate.

10

Time Management

If you sleep for the average eight hours a night, that only leaves you 960 minutes to get everything else done each day. Some of that time you will have to spend eating, drinking and fulfilling other physical needs. Time is a scarce and valuable commodity which you cannot afford to waste.

Try keeping a time log on yourself for a few days or weeks. It is a horrible experience, and because few of us can resist the temptation to lie to ourselves, I suggest you enlist the aid of your right-hand person, and ask her to keep the log for you.

You will then get an honest view of how much the 80/20 law (80 per cent of your time to do 20 per cent of the job) applies to you. Many of us fall into the trap of never having time to do things right, but always having to find time to do them again. It is a sign of inefficient management.

There are some simple rules in time management. First you've got to understand the difference between things which are **important**, things which are **urgent** and things which are **routine**.

The conflict arises when you find yourself dragged into doing the things which are urgent because there are deadlines involved, when they are not necessarily the most important things in terms of what you want to achieve.

The ideal is to have your right-hand person removing the urgent but unimportant jobs from your desk, and delegating them down the line. If a telephone call has to be returned by 9.30, then ask someone else to take care of it. That way you have dealt with the urgent job, but it hasn't taken up any of your important time.

The routine stuff will always be there, and this needs to be dealt with by appointment. It is the only way you will ever get it done amongst all the important and urgent things. Every day and every week, set aside some time for the routine tasks which cannot be left undone.

Tasks

You could divide your tasks into 'things that happen to you' and 'things that you make happen'. There are 'active, positive tasks', which are the things that you want to do because they are in line with your objectives, and there are 'reactive tasks' which are pushed onto you because someone else wants them done.

If you aren't careful the bulk of your time can be swamped with these reactive tasks as other people ask you to provide them with information or to attend meetings. Because you are a nice person you are always reacting to other people instead of controlling your own active tasks.

You must always schedule your time and control your diary closely. Don't let other people sneak things into it. Ask yourself with each task: 'Do I actually have to do this myself, or could one of my people handle it?'

Beware of pet subjects, we all have them. They are the things which we like doing most, so we keep on picking them up, even when we don't have to. They will eat into your time if you don't control them.

Making time to manage

You must make yourself time to manage instead of just 'doing things'. First of all learn to delegate. Only do things if only you can do them. Next you must train the people around you. Don't suddenly swamp them with work just because you are too busy to handle it or they'll do it wrong and then get upset. Train them how to do things properly.

Don't do two things at once, which is where the telephone becomes a problem. If you are in the middle of a report and you take a call you are being forced to divide your attentions, and that can only be bad.

Allocate sufficient time to each project. If it needs half an hour, then give it that much. If it is a big report which needs a couple of hours work, set aside that amount of time, don't try to do it in fifteen-minute bites, because you will be continually trying to remember where you were, and that will take twice as long.

Try to put people first. Your job is to lead them, and you will get a lot of feedback if you communicate with them in the right way. So make an appointment with your paperwork, but for the rest of the day put personal communications first.

Use money to save time

This is a form of delegation, but it means paying someone else to do the non-important jobs. If you are at a meeting and you find you have left a vital document at home, there is no point you driving all the way back for it, no matter how important it is. Send a courier, because the only skill needed is the ability to get there and back, while your skills can be better employed dealing with other matters at the meeting.

Many people have a horror of spending money on taxis instead of taking buses or trains, when they should be asking how much time they could be saving themselves. A manager's time is valuable, so don't hesitate to invest money in saving it.

Use the mornings and evenings

Every morning and evening there is a blissful lull, before the telephone starts ringing and after it stops. You can achieve more in those twenty-minute periods than you would in an hour at the peak of the day's activity.

At the end of each day, you can sit quietly and settle your mind about what has happened during the day. Make a list of the things that you need to do tomorrow, and leave it on your desk for the morning. You can then go home with a clear mind, not having to worry about remembering things when you wake up, and having literally left your work behind you.

Learn to use a dictating machine, since that will save your right-hand person having to sit patiently while you stare out of the window or take telephone calls. It also means you can dictate whenever you want, wherever you are.

So let's have another sign.

Take control of your time

BAF disease

This disease is named after the sort of 'Blue Assed Fly' which buzzes around in a state of permanent crisis, using up far too many resources to get the job done.

If people have to work overtime to get things ready by tomorrow, or you have to provide express delivery in order to get something delivered on time, you are suffering from BAF disease.

The chances are that all the crises were brought about in the first place by bad management planning and bad organization.

Sometimes, of course, people need a little time pressure in order to achieve good results and to get the adrenaline flowing, but are you sure that is the reason why you do it, or could it be simple disorganization?

A number of business surveys have indicated that the average manager works fifty to sixty hours a week. He takes work home with him and lives with a wife who has to struggle, often unsuccessfully, to keep him human. He then carries his work, often unfinished, back to the office where he will be interrupted every eight minutes by subordinates or other executives seeking advice or answers to problems. Most of these problems are things that other employees are being paid to resolve. He spends 80 per cent of his time communicating and only 20 per cent doing creative work, including thinking. The Chest and Heart Association say that this is fatal.

Time pressures can help some people with the creative aspects of management. Creativity is part of every manager's job, but it doesn't come naturally to most of us, we need to work at it.

First of all find your best time. Do you think better in the early morning or late at night? Next, find the best way for you. Some people like to lock themselves away in an office and put up the 'Do not disturb' sign. Others like to have people around them to bounce ideas off.

Try starting with a blank piece of paper and say to yourself: 'Right, I have to find a different way of doing this, a different way of solving the problem.' Some people are terrified of blank sheets of paper, in which case this won't work for them. For many people, however, it is a good starting point.

Everyone is different, and everyone has to find their own best way of working when they want to be creative.

Managing meetings

I have never yet attended a meeting which couldn't have been shorter by at least 50 per cent. They drag on because people's attention wanders and their spans of concentration vary. Somebody might start off fast and then ease off in the middle, coming back at the end, which means the meeting stretches out. In my experience any meeting that lasts sixty minutes is losing time from then on, and probably should have ended ten minutes earlier.

If you are in charge it is your job to make sure your meetings run efficiently.

A meeting should consist of between four and seven people. If you have more than that you should either split it into two or split the attendance so that some people attend part one and some part two.

Look at the order of the meeting on the agenda. Sometimes, if meetings have been going on in companies for ages, they have a set way of doing things, which often means putting all the boring bits at the beginning. But the beginning is the time when the members are at their freshest and most creative, so try putting the boring stuff at the end so it doesn't matter if some people fall asleep.

Sometimes the people who write the agendas seem to see it as a challenge to use as few words as possible to describe the items to be discussed, coming up with titles like 'Development Budget Item 3'. That's a mistake, since it merely leaves people in the dark. Always write a short sentence to give people a better idea of what it is you want to achieve. Are you planning to increase the budget, or cut it, or scrap it, or what?

At the same time you need to guard against the people who let their pens run away with them, creating reams of paper which nobody will have time to read. If it will help, then ask people to write summaries, but limit them to one side of one piece of paper. It is always possible to say what you want in two or three hundred words, and it's a good discipline to practise.

As chairman of the meeting you are the team leader. It is your job to get the best out of the rest. The people introducing topics on the agenda are your task leaders. You can't do both jobs yourself. If subjects come up in which you have a particular interest, you must delegate the introduction and debate to someone else, because your job as chairman is to remain impartial, to clarify, to assist progress and to bring a conclusion out of the group.

This is another occasion where a flip chart is useful. As you get into the discussion, capture the options as they arise so that when you come to summarize what's been going on you can see clearly what points have emerged. Otherwise people will lose track during the course of the debate.

The whole purpose of a committee is that you should be committed to the end conclusion wherever you started from. You may have come in with different opinions, but you all end up committed to what is decided. The chairman, therefore, has to sell all his members on the conclusions that they have reached. You have to encourage them and send them away feeling that they support the conclusions that were drawn.

Manager's time planning exercise

1   Decide how many hours you spend on work in an average week. Include travelling time: i.e. the hours from leaving to returning home.
2   In the spaces 1 to 10 below, list categories of tasks/activities which you expect to have to carry out at work in your next full working week.
3   In the hours column estimate how many hours you will be spending on each activity. To keep it simple – take it to the nearest half hour.

Activity	Hours in week	M/S/C	A/R	Revised hours
1				
2				
3				
4				
5				
6				
7				
8				
9				
10 Miscellaneous				
Total activities				

4   In the M/S/C column prioritize the tasks as 'must' 'should' or 'could'.
5   In the A/R column indicate whether the tasks are 'active' or 'reactive'. If over half your time is spent in reactive tasks, is there time to think?
6   Now imagine that you are told – quite unexpectedly – before the week begins that you have to attend a conference on the Thursday and Friday. You have no choice in this, and now only 60 per cent of your week is available. Something has to go. What will it be?
7   In the revised hours column write how long you will now spend on each task.

If you succeed in making those two days completely clear, use one of them for effective management and reward yourself with the other one. Play golf or something.

The game plan

Why are games usually more enjoyable than work? Because they provide what work doesn't provide. All games have:

1   A clear and meaningful **goal** to achieve.
2   A very simple **scoring system** so that everyone (players and spectators) can see at all times how they are doing.
3   A simple **do** and **don't** system of behaviour – the **rules** to win and to avoid losing an advantage.
4   A clear, certain, immediate and personal **reward** system.

Some 'games' you might play for yourself:

● Have half as many and half as long meetings.
● Cut interruptions by 50 per cent.
● Cut out memos altogether.
● Reduce boss imposed time – train the boss.
● Reduce colleague imposed time – go to *their* offices.
● Reduce subordinate imposed time – insulate but don't isolate yourself.
● Reduce system imposed time – cut it down or out.

- Hands on – once only – and do something with every piece of paperwork.
- Clear your desk at the end of each game you play.
- Use dead time (travelling, waiting) to good purpose.
- Vote for full employment – of your subordinates.
- Put off nothing till tomorrow that someone else can do today.
- Clean out your briefcase and use it only for visits to customers/suppliers.

Checklist

1 Try keeping a time chart.

2 Recognize the difference between important, urgent and routine tasks.

3 Keep 'reactive' tasks to the minimum.

4 Control your diary closely.

5 Delegate to give yourself more time to manage.

6 Train people to take over your workload effectively.

7 Allocate enough time to finish one job at a time.

8 Put people-communication first.

9 Invest money to save time.

10 Use the early mornings and evenings.

11 Shorten meetings.

12 Use time pressures creatively.

11
Leadership

A major part of good leadership is your attitude towards your people. Do you see them as employees, as staff, as the department, or do you see them as the team?

Your attitude toward them will affect how they look upon their jobs. If you get it wrong they might see themselves as:

The unwilling, led by the unknown, achieving the impossible for the ungrateful.

They could even be saying: 'We have done so much for so long with so little, we are now qualified to do anything with nothing.'

Those are typical attitudes of the unmotivated, unled mass of people who arrive at work at nine each morning, do their jobs and go home again at five in the evening.

If you are going to be a good leader that is not what you want. You want a team of people who are dedicated to achieving things, not just to working. Rather than 'employees' or 'staff', it might be better to refer to them as 'members of the company'. It might be technically incorrect, but at least it doesn't imply a 'them and us' approach to internal relations. Discrimination is never good if you are trying to create team spirit.

Good leaders must be aware all the time that they are human beings managing other human beings, not just pegs in holes. Human beings will always have problems, ambitions, crises, emotions and dramas. We are all individuals and we respond to private needs.

Working in an organization is very like having an account in a bank. You put money in and every now and again you need to draw it out. It is the same with your interrelationships with other people in the organization. For a lot of the time you are putting in, supporting others when they are miserable or don't feel well. You are helping them through an illness or a bereavement, buoying them up and giving them support. Then, every so often, it will be you who needs this support, and you can draw on the bank of good feeling. A leader who gives out this sort of care will be amazed by what he gets back when he needs it.

Most people fear change and will resist it. A leader, therefore, has to support his people and help them in the inevitable changes that they are going to face. At the beginning of this book we decided that 'if you aren't changing you aren't marketing'. The world is changing around us, and a good leader has to take his people through changes which they may find unsettling.

How to lead

Leadership is different from management. General Wavell once said: 'Men are governed through their emotions rather than their intelligences,' and that is a very important point. Leadership is emotional rather than intellectual.

Leaders are people who can persuade others to follow them, which means that they have to be at the front not the back. It is also a very personal thing. When you talk to people in commerce about leadership they often expect you to come up with a list of the 'dos and don'ts' of how to be a leader. But it is more individual than that. We are all different, and so each of us has a different style of leadership. You can't simply copy what a great leader does and expect to become one yourself.

Leadership, therefore, requires you to develop your own style, which requires freedom within the structure of the organization. All the best and strongest leaders have some personal idiosyncrasies, whether it be their style of dress or their mannerisms. There is nearly always something distinctive about them.

So a company has to have an organizational structure that allows for the development of individuals, with all their attendant idiosyncrasies.

In a book called *How to Manage*, Peter Prior, the chairman of Bulmers, says:

Leaders stand out by being different. They question assumptions and are suspicious of tradition. They seek out the truth and make decisions based on fact, not prejudice. They have a preference for innovation.

Leaders are observant and sensitive people. They know their team and develop mutual confidence within it. They state clear objectives and encourage a sense of security by defining territory for individual action. They delegate real authority. They do not interfere and they praise more often than they criticise. They are humble rather than dogmatic, humorous rather than earnest, diffident rather than over-bearing. They encourage initiative and ensure that success is recognised and rewarded.

I think that sums it up, and brings us to another sign.

> **As a leader you achieve your results through other people**

Generating team spirit

So how do leaders go about generating team spirit? First they've got to identify the team to themselves and to others. They've got to find some way of making it stand out – in colours, or clothes like ties and jackets, or premises identified with a sign. You give them a name that they can call themselves. It can be formal or informal – it can be Dave's Demons for a sales team or Valvologists for a group making and selling valves – as long as they can identify themselves with it, and can be identified by other people.

The leader must make a point of highlighting the successes within a team, using charts or graphs, with little presentations and fun ideas. Even small successes can be celebrated with a wooden spoon or a half pint down the pub at the end of the week. It doesn't matter what you do as long as you recognize success and keep the fun bubbling along.

A leader must accept blame, but he must reflect praise. If something goes wrong inside the team you take the blame and then you sort it out with the culprit, you don't pass the buck. If, on the other hand someone praises you for a brilliant job, you must say 'Ah yes, Fred did that, let's call him in so you can tell him yourself.'

The point is that if you want your team to be loyal to you, you must stick by them.

A leader must set targets, coach for results and then reward success. For a team to have spirit they must be working for something. Even if they are clerical workers doing mundane jobs, they can still have targets like the number of mistakes they don't make, or the number of

Illegible

documents they process in a day. There are always ways of setting
objectives.

You must praise people as often as possible, and thank them for their
efforts. Thank them when they do an ordinary job, and praise them
when they do something special. At the end of each week try saying:
'Thanks for doing your job this week. That was a good week. Thank
you for what you've done.'

Changing the pace of work

If you are going to engender a fresh spirit into a team, you have got to
make the business bustle. There are some ways of doing that which
you can start from day one. The first thing is always to be happy
yourself. Don't let them catch you looking like an old boot, always
look cheerful and confident. Try asking people cheery questions. If
they are looking happy themselves, ask them why.

It helps if you have a secret plan up your sleeve, because other people
will always sense it. If you haven't got a real one, then pretend you
have. Even if you haven't a clue how you are going to go about it all,
make them think you have a plan.

Next you should do something physical, as we mentioned earlier,
like knocking down a wall or moving the desks around.

Try to get people to innovate as often as possible, and be innovative
yourself.

Move fast around the office, as if you are bursting with energy, not
weighed down with the problems of the world. And make sure the
corners of your mouth are always turned *up*!

You can make yourself do all these things. It may be hard at the
beginning, particularly if you are starting with a demotivated team,
but it will soon start to come naturally, and you will find yourself
swept along by the enthusiasm of the other people you have inspired.

Delegation versus abdication

We have talked a lot about the importance of delegation, but a manager
must be able to differentiate between delegation and abdication. It
isn't just a question of passing the buck and foisting the blame onto

Delegation

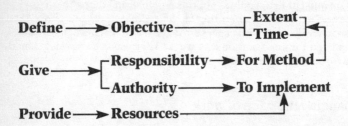

Figure 28

someone further down the line. You have to delegate in the right manner.

So start as shown in Figure 28 by defining the objectives, particularly the extent and timing of what you want someone to achieve. Then you must give your subordinate responsibility and authority. If you just make them responsible, all you are doing is sticking them with the blame. You must give them the necessary authority to achieve the required result.

You must also provide the resources they need for the job, whether it is time, money or equipment, and then you must monitor what they do, not leave them to drown. Monitoring does not mean interfering. It doesn't mean looking over their shoulders and telling them you 'wouldn't do it that way'. The purpose of monitoring is to stop them from failing. They must be successful if they are to learn and gain confidence. So you only help them if you absolutely must. But remember *you* are still accountable.

Styles of management

There are three styles of management: **consult**, **direct** and **suggest**. Consulting means asking the team what they think and then making decisions, which is a sort of democracy. Direct means you decide and you tell them: 'Do it'. Suggesting means that you don't actually tell them what to do, you just suggest it and let them choose whether they do it or not.

If you are evil you can do the suggesting, and then abdicate all responsibility if the thing goes wrong: 'I never told him to do that!'

A good manager uses a mixture of all three of these styles at the appropriate moments. Style is a very important element of management, and anyone wanting to get to the top would be well advised to put a lot of study into it.

I would like to end this chapter with a few of the most important words and phrases which managers must be able to say:

- 'I admit I made a mistake.'
- 'You did a good job.'
- 'What's your opinion?'
- 'Would you mind?'
- 'Thank you'
- 'We'

The one word a good manager should avoid using is 'I'.

Checklist

1 Develop the right attitude towards other people.
2 Create an environment which encourages individuality.
3 Deliberately build team spirit.
4 Create a positive and dynamic mood.
5 Delegate but don't abdicate responsibility.
6 Develop a management style to suit the job.

12
Motivation

We all know that incentives are symbolized by carrots and sticks. You either offer people more money, or you threaten them with the sack. A lot of sales managers, however, still seem to be figuring out which end to apply the carrot! For most people, particularly those under the age of fifty-four, carrots are always more effective than sticks. But motivation consists of more than these two symbols.

We all have a differing number of needs. There are the universal ones like houses, food, drink and transport. Everyone has to have these basics to survive. Above these you have the possessions which people want, even if they don't strictly need them. It might be a caravan or a boat, or an extension to the house.

From the 'want to have', you move on to the 'want to be', with all our ego-needs and the self-images which we have. We all want to impress somebody, even if it's only our families. In many cases we want to belong to certain cliques, which require money or status for membership.

We also need to achieve things, and to be seen to achieve them by our spouses, our colleagues and our bosses, and we need to grow for our own fulfilment.

All motivation is internal, not external, and sometimes we might want to grow sideways, broadening our abilities, rather than upwards.

Some of us are driven by only one or two of these basic needs, others by a mixture of all of them. The manager has to identify which ones apply to which individuals.

Management guru Douglas McGregor gave us two theories about organizations. In Theory X he claimed that people hate work, and that they have to be driven or threatened to get them to work towards organizational objectives. They like security and are unambitious. They want to be told what to do and they dislike responsibility.

Sadly, the majority of organizations work on this basis. All the most successful companies, however, work on Theory Y.

McGregor's Theory Y says that people don't hate work, that it's as natural as rest or play. They don't have to be forced or threatened, and if they commit themselves to mutual objectives they'll drive themselves more effectively than you can drive them, but they will only commit themselves as long as they can see ways of satisfying their ego and development needs.

Once you have recognized what these needs are, Theory Y will go like a train. Your carrots, therefore, have got to be the right ones. You will have to look at each one and judge its effectiveness for each individual.

Money is obviously an important carrot, but it usually has a fairly low ceiling – around 20 per cent more than covering basic 'have' needs and money ceases to motivate most people. So let's look at the non-financial factors.

There is a long list of possible non-financial motivating factors including: a sense of belonging, achievement, success, a sense of importance, responsibility, satisfaction, competition, fear, force, job security, help, encouragement, praise, interest, respect, involvement, example, training, ambition, trust, change, stress, team spirit, pride, status, variety, communication, job enrichment and power.

You could also add the fact that people will work harder to please the boss, but only if they respect the boss.

The trouble with money

Motivating only with money is often only partially effective because it is like a switchback. If the basic cost of living rises; then people will be motivated by fear, the fear of having less and not being able to manage.

Once you get to 20 per cent above the basic cost of living, the 'have' needs, however, you are moving into the possessions motivation sector. Money will motivate sometimes, but at others will be completely useless. Take a typical young bachelor. He is motivated at a very low level by money because he's got enough to pay the rent, buy the beer and can live on his expense account with his company car. He doesn't want to grow any more, he is quite happy. He is consequently very hard to motivate. He comes to work from a different direction each morning!

Then he meets 'the' girl, falls in love and they both start planning a home, which costs a lot of money. Provided he's got some sort of commission element in his package, his motivation will suddenly shoot up. You haven't done anything different, but he is suddenly working flat out.

So they get married and buy a house and furnish it, all of which takes a few years, and then suddenly he hits another plateau, because with their combined incomes they've now got enough to live on. Again you will have trouble motivating him just with money.

Then she gets pregnant, and he's off again planning for nurseries and all the rest, and worrying about how they will manage when she has to give up work. He works flat out for a while, until the baby arrives and then he is too exhausted to perform at his best and he slows down again for three years or so.

They decide that one's enough and she goes back to work and if you are unlucky he might plateau off and settle into the same rut for the rest of his life. If you are lucky, however, he will start wanting something different now, like a boat or a set of golf clubs, or anything that will get him out of the house.

So, until he gets whatever it is he wants, his efforts shoot up again, and you can see that over his whole career the effect of money on his motivation has gone up and down like a roller coaster. So if you want to motivate with money, you must monitor each individual's circumstances regularly, so that you can tell when they will and will not respond.

The system shown in Figure 29 was devised by Abraham Maslow,

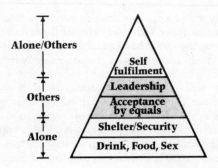

Figure 29

who says that people at the basic level have the basic needs, without which we would all die, like drink, food and sex. For some people that is all they need or want, and they will remain happily at the bottom of the pile.

The second level is shelter and security, which could be the bachelor pad, or the nice little family house.

Then comes acceptance by equals, which means the social element of their lives, including coffee mornings and dinner parties, clubs or whatever is important to them. Most people in selling should be 'people people' and should, therefore, be operating at this level.

Above that, you have leadership and the aspirations of the few at the top of the pile. As you reach the top of the peak it gets lonelier. Maslow calls this the self-fulfilment or self-actualization level.

On the two bottom layers of the pyramid you can operate completely alone, as an individual. By the time you get to the two layers of acceptance by equals and leadership you need other people to make it work. When you get right to the top you can do it the people way, or it can be lonely.

No matter how high you rise, however, it is the lower levels which take priority if anything goes wrong. If it has been a bad year and you have to get sales up fast, you might need to threaten somebody with the sack unless certain increases are achieved. You are immediately threatening their shelter and security, and the person under threat will stop worrying about his leadership and acceptance roles, and will concentrate on surviving until the crisis is past.

Some people, of course, might react to such a threat by starting to read the job ads, others might go down to the security level and then not come back up again, meaning that all their managerial input to the company goes out of the window. They go to pieces under the pressure, constantly worrying and moaning until colleagues start actively avoiding them. Some descend even lower than the threatened level and resort to food, drink and sex – not necessarily in that order!

Incentive schemes

The best incentive scheme I ever came across was in the late sixties at a distributor of electronic components in Reading, called Celdis Ltd. The Sales Director bought an old Silver Cloud Rolls Royce for about £1,500.

He then introduced a scheme for his ten people which worked monthly over a year. Each month there was a winner who could trade in his Cortina for the Rolls, using it to make all his business calls. At the end of the month he went to the bottom of the list and didn't get another crack until month eleven or twelve. So the two top guys had the opportunity of winning two months, and everyone else had the chance of winning at least one month. There was, however, a slight stigma attached to being the last one to make it.

Within four months they had won so much publicity with the idea within the trade that customers were ringing up and asking when their rep was going to have the Roller, so that they could have a ride. The answer to that was: 'When you give him enough business to win his chance.'

The scheme had all the necessary ingredients of a good incentive. It was unusual, it gained publicity, the customers were involved, the salespeople's spouses were turned on by the thought of having a Rolls in the drive, and it gave everyone a chance to win during the period of the scheme, which is vital. At the end of the year they sold the car and liquidated their costs.

Many companies, of course, use more modest cars as incentives. The bigger engines, or better extras can all be used as steps up the motivation ladder. Management have to be sure, however, that they will have the nerve to take the better cars away from the people again if their performance drops, otherwise they are wasting time and money and will lose the respect of their team.

Things like bigger and better cars don't just motivate the salespeople, they also motivate their spouses, and raise their status in the eyes of the neighbours.

Awarding titles

Titles also motivate people, and please their families. In the 1960s a confectionary wholesaler, selling into retail shops, wasn't happy with the volume of business his five-strong sales team was producing. So he sold their Austin A40s, bought them 2.4 Jaguars and gave them business cards which said Sales Director.

His sales volume multiplied tenfold within the year. He had raised the status of his team in the eyes of the customers, so they were more willing to stop and talk, and he had given the reps the confidence to ask for big orders and to work more responsibly.

The league table

Results at end of month - 8				Area Manager's current estimate for rest of year		
Salesperson	Original agreed annual target	Turnover achieved so far	Balance left to achieve	Will make balance on nose	Will sell more than balance by	Will sell less than balance by
ANDREWS, J.	150,000	98,000	52,000	/		
ARNOLD, P.	150,000	122,000	28,000	/		
BEASLEY, G.	110,000	108,000	2,000		25,000	
BREWSTER, M.	110,000	85,000	25,000	/		
CARVER, D.	84,000	61,000	23,000	/		
EVANS, D.	110,000	73,000	37,000			20,000
GILLMAN, R.	140,000	80,000	60,000			25,000
JACOBS, E.	125,000	123,000	2,000		35,000	
KEITH, B.	80,000	58,000	22,000		5,000	
McEWAN, J.	86,000	35,000	51,000			33,000
NORMAN, L.	150,000	105,000	45,000	/		
ONIONS, P.	127,000	90,000	37,000			17,000
PACKER, A.	165,000	122,000	43,000		10,000	
PORTER, J.	130,000	70,000	60,000			30,000
ROBERTS, G.	55,000	36,000	19,000	/		
SUTCLIFFE, S.	102,000	75,000	27,000			7,000
TAYLOR, B.	60,000	37,000	23,000		7,000	
THOMPSON, P.	110,000	79,000	31,000		2,000	
VINCENT, W.	100,000	85,000	15,000		18,000	
WATSON, J.	150,000	110,000	40,000		5,000	

All figures rounded up or down to nearest 1000.

Figure 30

Figure 30 is an example of a league table designed to be a motivational tool. The example is for a larger sales force with several area managers who also need motivating. You will see that it gives an alphabetical list of all the sharp end people in the company concerned. It lists their originally agreed annual targets, and is updated each month. So that at any given time you can see the turnover achieved so far, and the balance left to achieve.

Never give individuals their own results while keeping all the others secret. Everybody likes to see how they are doing compared to the rest.

The key to the table is in the last three columns which are the manager's estimates of how each of his people is going to perform for the rest of the year. Will they hit their targets? Will they sell more? If so, by how much? Will they sell less? If so, how much less?

Every month each manager has to take each of his salespeople and go over the rest of the year in detail with them, agreeing with them what should be put on the table. That way it is the managers who are being judged on the accuracy of the table, as well as the people at the sharp end.

Competitions

Competitions to improve sales can be dangerous traps because they can lead a company to be too single minded. To illustrate the danger of single mindedness, let me tell you a true story, about a company in Sheffield that had a problem. I was called in to help sort things out, to be greeted by a very worried Managing Director, who informed me

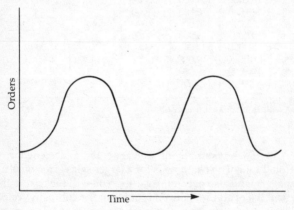

Figure 31

that the company had a rather pronounced seasonal demand. The order intake graph looked like Figure 31.

As the products were highly diversified, from chains, pallets, fabrications and tanks to Goliath cranes, I was quite intrigued by the thought of a seasonal demand of such regularity and proportions, so I started digging.

It took all of three weeks to get to the root of the problem – and it will take five years at least to correct it and put the company back on an even keel. Here's what happened.

At a time just a few months before the end of a particular financial year, the Managing Director, an accountant and also the major shareholder, generated himself a complex about takeovers. He'd lie in his bath with the adrenaline pounding through his body, reading the *Financial Times*, worrying about the state of his company and imagining that it was ripe for a swift bid from the competition.

The complex grew to overpowering proportions, so much so that the Managing Director started figuring how much he'd get for his shareholding when the takeover came about.

'Not enough,' he reckoned. So he set about reshaping the asset and financial position of the company. 'What we need is a fatter order book,' he decided. 'That'll put the asking price up a bit.'

So he called the Sales Manager into his office. 'George,' he said, 'we need more orders before the end of the year. Get your salespeople to

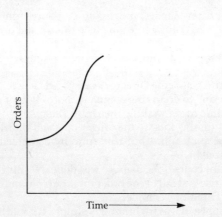

Figure 32

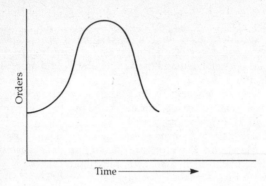

Time ⟶

Figure 33

drop whatever they're doing and concentrate on securing firm orders. I want to see the order book full by December 31.'

This sounded reasonable to George, so he phoned all his salespeople to pass on the necessary instructions, and the order graph shot up (Figure 32).

By the time the graph had reached its first peak, the Managing Director had forgotten all about his complex. Faced with such an increase in business he was busy choosing a new yacht for next summer.

He called the Sales Manager into his office, poured him a whisky and said 'George, you're doing a fine job. Keep this up and there's a seat on the Board for you.'

Shortly afterwards the order intake graph plummeted downwards (see Figure 33).

Hysterical, the Managing Director again faced George. 'I don't know what you're trying to do to this company, but if it isn't rectified fast, now's a good time to start taking the *Daily Telegraph*.'

A swift, stimulating kick to the salespeople and shortly afterwards, up went the graph again – but this time by coincidence, not with malice aforethought.

By this time of course, the damage was done. Nothing, but nothing could stop the rise and fall of the order intake graph, and all because of the Managing Director's complex.

What had happened was frighteningly simple. It could happen to any company for many different reasons.

Given the initial instruction to drop everything else and concentrate on getting in the orders, every single person on the sales force was doing the same thing at the same time – chasing up all the outstanding quotations (the only way to get orders quickly in industrial selling).

They succeeded in closing quite a few sales. Not all of them, but enough to send the graph rocketing upwards.

Which was fine – until they ran out of outstanding quotations. Then they had to spend a period of time generating fresh enquiries to get to quotation stage. During this period, very few orders could be secured, so down came the graph again.

You see, every product has a cycle time – the time it takes on average to generate an enquiry and process it to the point where the order is placed.

This cycle is exceptionally hard to change. So if an entire sales force does the same thing at the same time, the result is a similar-sized reaction at some future point in the cycle.

That is what competitions tend to encourage. If you have a range of products and you want to run contests, don't run them throughout the company or throughout the range. Overlap your product life cycles or gestation periods. Run different contests at different times of the year for different products.

Personal recognition

This is another key ego motivator. The essence is captured in those two little words which you sometimes see on the top of Berni House steaks, 'Well done'.

So many managers find it hard to praise their people. You must try to catch them doing something right, rather than always trying to catch them doing something wrong.

It is always best to say 'Well done' publicly at a team meeting. Equal best is to write a personal letter and send it to the person's home, so that he opens it over breakfast with his wife, who also reads it.

Dear Bill,

I was delighted to see the Thompson order come in today. Knowing what you are up against, you must be feeling on top of the world. Well done. I'll see to it that they get delivery on the nose.

Regards

Show them that they have pleased the boss – they will respond.
Let's finish with a sign:

> **Motivate in the future**

That means don't ever reward someone until you have received the
results you want. The reward must always be at the end. If you give it
at the beginning everything will stop after a month, when they forget
that they ever received it. In fact they will have come to look on the
reward as their due rather than an extra. Remember – the only place
where reward comes before work is in the dictionary.

Checklist

1   Find out what motivates each individual on your team.
2   Work out when each is likely to need more money.
3   Be inventive with your incentives, and involve everyone.
4   Think about your people's titles.
5   Try putting together a league table.
6   Use competitions with care.
7   Never miss a chance to praise.

13

Unlucky for Some

There is nearly always a difference between what we are and what we are perceived to be. Have you, for instance, got any of the nasty little habits which annoy you in other people? Do you scratch your bum or pick your nose? Are your jokes dreadful or your manners revolting? Think of all the things that drive you mad in other people, and then see if they apply to you.

You must have at least some of them. Once you have identified which, you can set about putting them right.

There are people who believe they are perfect, of course. No doubt you have met some of them. If you are one, it might be worth having an honest talk with your spouse, secretary or loved one. You will find that very revealing. It could mean the end of a beautiful friendship, but do it anyway.

So change your habit profile, which means getting rid of the bad habits and starting some new habits. You could begin, for instance, by starting your day earlier, because it is undoubtedly true that the early birds get the fattest worms. You might try being old fashioned about some things, because that can be very pleasing to a lot of people.

Your habits are just one part of your image. Just as you can change your habits, you can change your image to be whatever you want, without losing your soul.

You might choose to conform to the corporate image. Every company has one to some degree. It is either large or it is small, old and steadfast or young and revolutionary. It's bustling and dynamic or sleepy and trustworthy. You can dress to fit the company picture, or you could create an image of your own which will make you stand out from the crowd.

At one time everyone at IBM wore a white shirt and grey suit and that's a very successful company, but remember what we were saying earlier about individuality, idiosyncrasies and leadership.

Before you decide whether to change or not, you have to know what image you are putting over at the moment. Do you look like an elder statesman, or a young whizz-kid? Be honest with yourself. Once you have decided, you can change a number of things, like the way you move and the way you dress. Most of us dress the way we do as the result of childhood conditioning, but that is not necessarily the best basis for deciding the image you want to project to the world twenty or thirty years later.

So don't settle for being what you are. Start thinking about what you would like to be. Look in the mirror and ask yourself: 'Would I trust this person with a million pounds worth of business?'

Ambition

I am one of those people who believes that most of us can be whatever we want to be. If you want to be something like Prime Minister it might be difficult because of the waiting list, but in reasonable terms you can certainly make yourself into the sort of person you want to be.

Most people, however, simply don't know what it is they want, so there is no way that they can achieve it. You must decide what your goal is before you can go for it.

It can be a modest ambition, or it can be a surprising one, but the first thing to do is fix it into your mind and you will find that after a while it will start to tow you along with it.

Get yourself prepared for it, with all the necessary bits of experience, training and qualifications, so that when the opportunity arrives you are ready to take it, and have all the cards in your hand.

If you find that you are failing to achieve your ambition – some of us simply haven't got the brains to be nuclear physicists or the voice to be Frank Sinatra – then don't be afraid to rethink and find another ambition. If you don't do that, and simply allow yourself to fail, you will become disillusioned, bitter and miserable, and that is the start of the big downward spiral in both health and happiness. If you don't like the way your plans are working out, then change them.

Health

Nobody can be successful if they don't have good health. It is hard enough to reach the top if you are in the peak of condition, so don't handicap yourself by not looking after your body. No one expects you to stick to a rigid diet of nut cutlets and hours of aerobics each morning, but there are some practical steps which you can take.

Let's take an example of a group of people travelling to an overseas exhibition. They all catch the last plane out of Britain, which is the sort of thing a lot of business people do, and arrive late at the hotel. Because they are late they get the rooms which are sandwiched between the lift shaft and the tram cars, so that's their sleep gone for the whole week before they've started.

Anyway, the moment they arrive they shout: 'We're abroad', and head straight for the dodgiest part of town. They eat a fairly bad meal and drink some rough plonk and pay a high price, and don't get back to their sleepless beds until about three in the morning. From the first morning of the exhibition they're dead. They can't hope to sparkle and give their best on a stand for twelve hours feeling as they do, and they will never get enough rest to make them feel any better.

Wouldn't they enjoy themselves more if they took it steadily at the beginning, had a successful exhibition, and celebrated their success at the end by staying up all night?

Relaxation is enormously important, since overwork is the single largest factor in executive inefficiency. Make yourself relax, no matter how hard you find it. Take up a hobby. Whether it is building model aeroplanes or jogging doesn't matter. Business is a long-term game, and if you want to stay through to the end you don't want to burn yourself out in your twenties.

Moving up the ladder

When you feel restless and ready to move on, rather than immediately turning to the job pages of the *Sunday Times*, why not go job hunting inside your own company? It is often much easier, yet few people organize themselves to do it.

The first rule is to get your department running well without you, which means delegation. I've sat through so many meetings where people are looking for someone to promote, and they rule out all the best candidates because they can't afford to take them away from their present jobs.

Next you must cultivate the people in the department you want to move to. In many companies the different departments don't speak to each other, but if you want to work in 'International', you had better go and find out what they do, even if that just means drinking in the same pub. Unless they know who you are they won't think of you when a vacancy comes up.

Volunteer for things that will move you in the right direction. It shows you are keen and interested and again it brings you to the attention of others.

One of the companies I know of wanted to make a management promotion. There were two young fellows in the company who were equally ideal for the job, and as far as the managers could tell neither of them was thinking about it, they were both perfectly happy doing what they were doing. So neither of them got the job.

Now there is nothing wrong with being happy with your lot in life, if you have got as far as you want to go. If you want to get to the top, however, make sure the right people know about it. The company will always prefer to fill vacancies from inside where possible. By promoting people internally the company knows exactly what sort of person it is dealing with, someone who knows the business, is loyal and tested, and it saves them all the trouble of advertising and recruiting, with the attendant risks of making mistakes.

Luck

The one other ingredient of success which we all need is luck. But what *is* luck? I think the best description of it I've ever encountered gives us our final sign – but this time it is more a signpost! Luck, you see, isn't abstract, it's a place.

> **Luck is a place where preparation meets opportunity**

I hope that in this book I have given you some of the tools which you need to take you along the right road, towards the opportunities which you will undoubtedly find in the future.

Checklist

1	Change your habits for the better.
2	Decide what you want from life.
3	Make your image fit your ambition.
4	Look after your health and relax.
5	Look for internal promotions.
6	Be prepared for opportunities.

Answers to the 'managing or doing' test on page 93

1 **Doing**   This may be a highly necessary activity but it is selling, not managing. The direct purpose of the call is not to get results through others.

2 **Managing**   This is training.

3 **Doing**   This is selling.

4 **Managing**   This is supervising, assuming the manager does not have his people come to him for routine solutions to recurring problems which they are capable of handling. It would be counselling if a more formal personal discussion were needed.

5 **Doing**   The actual filling out of the form is clerical. Instructing your secretary how to fill it out would be a managing activity in that it would be delegating.

6 **Doing**   This may be an essential activity but the manager is actually performing a personnel function in the same way that he is selling when he calls upon an account. When he is actually interviewing he is not getting results through others. Deciding to hire someone after all the recruitment and selection has been done, however, would be considered a managing activity.

7 **Managing**   This is communicating, probably in order to develop a selling programme. It could also be a form of motivation.

8 **Doing**   The manager is developing objectives – which is a managing activity – but he is not delegating. He is developing objectives by account which his salespeople should be best qualified to do themselves. If he were to review the sales objectives of one of his salespeople then he would be managing.

9 **Managing**   This is planning. Compiling the budget in its proper form would be clerical.

10 **Managing** This is measuring and evaluating.

11 **Managing** This is developing the organization structure.

12	**Doing**	This is a methods engineering function. Deciding to implement an improved office layout would be a managing activity.
13	**Managing**	This is developing objectives as well as standards of performance.
14	**Managing**	This is taking corrective control action.
15	**Managing**	This is developing a programme of marketing strategy to achieve group results.

Index

Derek Wilson

Rothschild: A Story of Wealth and Power

The name synonymous with wealth, sophistication and power for generations – derived from the red shield (*rot schild*) which adorned the home of the family's founder Mayer Amschel, in the oppressed and crowded ghetto of eighteenth-century Frankfurt.

At first dependent on the whims of petty princelings, the Rothschilds accrued enormous political influence by backing governments, financing wars and orchestrating fiendishly complex international deals. They bought the Suez Canal for Disraeli, financed the Battle of Waterloo and arranged indemnity of 5,000 million frs. for France to pay Bismarck.

With lively anecdote, extensive interviews with members of the family and much previously unpublished material, Derek Wilson shows how the great bankers came to shape history, and became known throughout Europe for their prolific achievements in art, science, wine and charity. He also outlines the problem of ensuring the continuation of a dynasty.

Derek Wilson eloquently examines the continuing phenomenon of a family that has survived and triumphed over most major events and crises of the last two centuries.

'The Rothschild family is a marvellous subject, and Derek Wilson's masterly study is more than equal to it.' *Daily Telegraph*

'Erudite, unsycophantic and intensely readable.' *Books*

Donald Cameron Watt

How War Came

Panoramic in scope, flawless in presentation, this book is a monument of international history. Having amassed all that is known of the kaleidoscopic blunders, deceptions and fateful games of secret intelligence, Donald Watt cogently explains how Europe's leaders were influenced and misled by Hitler's demonic drive for power. Here, fascinatingly rearranged for the general reader, are the reasons for a multicausal war that reshaped the world.

'If you have only time to read one book on how the greatest war in history came about, Donald Watt has provided it' *Alan Bullock*

'Magnificent narrative history, a book so effortlessly readable that the years of diligent research on which it is based are in danger of being overlooked' *The Listener*

'It is a life's work, in that it sums up the author's forty years of reading in the archives of the continent's foreign offices. It is also an unquestionable masterpiece, magnificently organised, beautifully written, and certain to be read for as long as people seek to explain the European tragedy of 1939' *John Keegan, Books of the Year, Daily Telegraph*

'It's a very good book indeed – the best, I think, on the subject' *Norman Stone, Professor of Modern History, Oxford University*

Peter Drucker

The New Realities

Challenging, insightful and provocative, *The New Realities* anticipates the central issues of a rapidly changing world. Some have already begun to take effect: the information-based organisation; the social function of management; the transnational economy; the increasing impotence of military and political power of arms; the democratisation of the Soviet Republic, and the disappearance of Roosevelt's America.

In almost every arena of politics, economics, business, government and society, Peter Drucker analyses the new realities to come. Already the bestselling author of many books on management and economics, he has innumerable followers. Now turning to address the changing demands of a postbusiness society, its government, leadership and economic direction, the broad-ranging theme and vision of *The New Realities* will win him many more.

M. R. D. Foot

S.O.E.

*The dirty tricks department of the British
Secret Service*

Recruited from remarkably diverse callings, the men
and women who were members of this most secret
agency lived in great and constant danger. Their job
was to support and stimulate resistance behind
enemy lines: their credentials fortitude, courage,
immense patience and a devotion to freedom.

The influence of SOE was felt all over the world.
Abyssinian tribesmen, American newsmen, French
farmers, exiled Russian grandees, coolies, rubber
workers, even the regent of Siam, smugglers,
printers, policemen, telephonists, tycoons, pros-
titutes, railwaymen and peasants from the Pyrenees
to the Balkans and beyond – all had a part to play as
saboteurs, informers, partisans or secret agents.

Fifty years after SOE's conception, its eminent
historian M. R. D. Foot now sheds fresh light on this
heroic force – a force so effective that it even made a
profit during its short but almost legendary
existence.

Hugo Cornwall

Datatheft

Computer fraud, industrial espionage and information crime

Datatheft, the undetectable crime that grows wherever new opportunities exist.

Datatheft, the typical computer criminal is not the genius programmer or hacker, but the middle-ranking, apparently loyal employee with inside knowledge.

Datatheft, computer fraud is a problem that goes to the heart of management responsibility. Read this book – you may never know what you're missing.

Datatheft, bestselling author of the controversial *Hacker's Handbook* Hugo Cornwall, a computer security consultant, is uniquely qualified to describe the nature of the crime that has no discernible parameters. Even in law it is an area of lightest grey.

Chris Ryder

The RUC: a Force Under Fire

According to Interpol, Northern Ireland is the most dangerous place in the world for a policeman. The RUC costs £1 million a day to operate, and in the last twenty years has seen over 250 of its members killed and more than 8,000 injured. Amazingly, there are almost twenty times more applicants than vacancies in the force whose techniques and expertise are emulated worldwide.

Journalist and Ulsterman Chris Ryder tells the inside story of the men and women whose courage and disregard for danger are almost routine. Authoritatively impartial, he traces the turbulent and increasingly complex history of the force.

The RUC covers the controversial use of plastic bullets, the innovative management style of Kenneth Newman, the ill-starred Stalker affair and the continuing ramifications of the Anglo-Irish Agreement. For all those interested in the more notorious terrorist and paramilitary groups of the sectarian divide, *The RUC* is required reading.

'Chris Ryder's book will help those who are concerned to move along the road to a peaceful Northern Ireland' *Merlyn Rees*

Tessa Blackstone & William Plowden

Inside the Think Tank
Advising the Cabinet 1971–1983

Its job was to 'think the unthinkable'

Set up by Edward Heath – abolished by Mrs Thatcher, the tiny apolitical hybrid known as the Central Policy Review Staff (or Think Tank) was a most inspired brainchild of British Government. Brilliantly directed at the start by the quirky and charismatic Lord Rothschild, it was created to encourage Ministers to anticipate future difficulties before they loomed into reality.

Taking a key role in the development of the policies of successive governments, the Think Tank was a remarkably prescient authority. Among its most significant successes were its ground-breaking report on the car industry and its accurate forecasts of economic and industrial problems, ranging from oil prices to unemployment.

However, the Think Tank was also involved in some highly publicised rows over nuclear power, public spending cuts, the Foreign Office, and the possible dismantling of the National Health Service. On returning to power in 1983 Mrs Thatcher decided to dispense with it, because it did not suit her style of government.

Both distinguished Think Tank members themselves, Tessa Blackstone and William Plowden tell the inside story of this extraordinary institution and make an excellent case for its reinvention.

'Probably the most important account of the workings of Whitehall since Richard Crossman's diaries' *The Economist*

David Lamb

The Africans

Africa is a continent of surprises, nothing is ever quite as it seems and nothing ever happens quite as it is supposed to.

Part political travelogue and part contemporary history, this book is the result of four years spent in Africa by the *Los Angeles Times* correspondent. David Lamb bounced from wars to *coups*, travelling through forty-eight countries and over 300,000 miles, interviewing witch doctors and presidents, guerrilla leaders and university professors, shanty town dwellers and slick entrepreneurs, seeking always to capture and to understand the contradictions of this diverse continent and its many peoples, caught between the mistakes of the past and the possible calamities of tomorrow.

'The best general survey of contemporary Africa now available.' *The Times Educational Supplement*